ARTISTS OF THE NATIONAL LIBRARY OF AUSTRALIA

OLIVE COTTON

With essays by Helen Ennis and Sally McInerney
And commentary by Olive Cotton

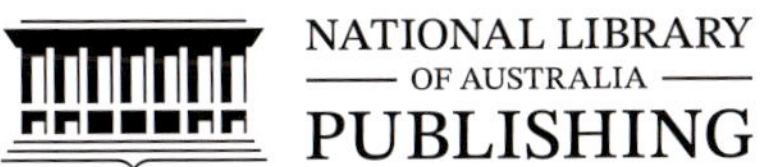

Published by National Library of Australia Publishing
Canberra ACT 2600

ISBN: 9781922507839

The National Library of Australia acknowledges Australia's First Nations Peoples—the First Australians—as the Traditional Owners and Custodians of this land and gives respect to the Elders—past and present—and through them to all Australian Aboriginal and Torres Strait Islander people.

Publisher: Lauren Smith
Managing editors: Amelia Hartney and Rosalind Clarke
Designer: Stan Lamond
Image coordinator: Madeleine Warburton

Printed in China by Asia Pacific Offset on FSC®-certified paper.

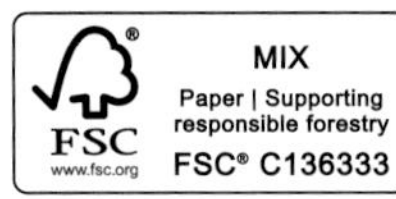

Find out more about NLA Publishing at nla.gov.au/national-library-publishing.
A catalogue record for this book is available from the National Library of Australia.

Foreword

This is a new edition of a book first published in 1995, following a period of rediscovery of Olive Cotton's art photography. *Olive Cotton, Photographer* contributed to solidifying Cotton's standing as one of the leading Australian modernist photographers. Importantly, it combined the voices of Cotton and her daughter, award-winning photographer and writer Sally McInerney, with that of acclaimed academic, curator and writer (now Professor Emeritus, Australian National University) Helen Ennis, to give a deeper sense than ever before of Cotton's creative story, her artistic impetus, approach and subject matter (portraiture and landscapes). This book repositioned the work of the unassuming Cotton firmly in Australian art history, after a 'lost' period of nearly forty years, during which Cotton had raised a family in country New South Wales.

Nearly thirty years on, it is important to note that this book also represents a moment in the development of Ennis's curatorial and personal relationship with Cotton. Ennis's role in the emergence of Cotton and her work continued beyond the publication of this book. She went on to curate with Judy Annear at the Art Gallery of New South Wales the hugely popular retrospective exhibition *Olive Cotton*, which further illuminated Cotton's output. The exhibition travelled on to the National Library, drawing tens of thousands of people to see Cotton's deft use of shadow and light in her black and white prints, superb technical skills, emotionally evocative and unpretentious photographs. In 2019, Ennis's relationship with Cotton's work and life culminated in the publishing of her biography of the photographer, offering further depth of insight and understanding of a complex and egalitarian photographer.

This book represents the beginning of a period of conscious collecting of women photographers' work by the National Library to help redress the unbalanced nature of research into the history of Australian photography. At the time of first publishing, Olive Cotton and Sally McInerney generously donated fifty-five prints to the Library. Those images are complemented here by thirteen from the National Gallery of Australia.

The Library's photographic collection today extends to over one million photographs.

Nicki Mackay-Sim
Director, Curatorial & Collection Research

Patterns in time

Helen Ennis

The essay below was written in 1995 when this book was first published. In the last years of Olive Cotton's life, she received considerable acclaim. Her work was the subject of a retrospective exhibition curated by Helen Ennis for the Art Gallery of New South Wales, Sydney, in 2000. The exhibition toured to the National Library of Australia. Cotton died in 2003 at the age of 92 and was buried at Morongla Creek Cemetery in central western New South Wales. Helen Ennis's biography, Olive Cotton: A Life in Photography, *was published by Fourth Estate, Sydney, in 2019.*

Once every fortnight, Olive Cotton spends two days in the small New South Wales town of Cowra, twenty-five kilometres from her home at Spring Forest, Koorawatha. These days and the night in-between have become part of a ritual that has work at its heart. For it is in Cowra that Cotton's darkroom is located; set up in 1964 with the help of family and friends, it was the hub of her practice as a professional photographer whose subject was country-town life. Now, no longer taking on clients:

> *I can come in early one morning ... and I can work all that day and stay at a nearby motel at night and get up early the next morning and come in again.*[1]

1 Olive Cotton in *Light Years,* a film about her life and work by Kathryn Millard (Lexicon Films, 1991).

The work that Cotton has devoted herself to since the early 1980s is printing, the second half of the photographic act. Between 1946—when she settled in the Cowra district with husband Ross McInerney—and the opening of her studio in 1964, Cotton had no access to darkroom facilities. But photography offers a generous deferment to those who, for whatever reason, need time to unite the two component parts of taking the negative and making the print. Though busy with farm and family life—daughter Sally was born in 1946 and son Peter followed two years later—Cotton continued taking photographs:

> *always with the feeling that one day I would have the chance to make the prints myself instead of just getting little contact prints from Kodak that I used as reference.*[2]

The concerted printing program of the last fifteen years has yielded hundreds of prints—from both old and new negatives. With the materialisation of each individual photograph, Cotton's oeuvre has taken on a fuller form. An overview has become possible, and a tying together of some of the main threads running through more than sixty years of photographic work.

Quite rightly, Cotton's photographs, singly and together, are now the centre of attention; they should not, however, be taken as the only measure of 'success'. Cotton's use of photography has been idiosyncratic for it has not been inevitably oriented towards outcomes. It is her ways of working that are also significant because they illuminate the value of work itself—as a process rather than simply as an end result. Through her photography, a sense of continuum is conveyed, akin to a journey in which the travel to a destination is as significant as the arrival.

From Cotton's perspective, working well involves time above all else—'time to think and time to concentrate', a fulsome expanse of 'unbroken time'.[3] Inextricably bound to this is solitude, which many artists also regard as a prerequisite for creative work. In the words of Australian sculptor Rosalie Gascoigne:

> *An artist's primary concern should be truth to self. To achieve this takes the best of one's time and effort ... in solitude ...* [artists] *get nearer to what they intrinsically have to offer.*[4]

---

2 *Light Years*, op. cit.
3 Ibid.
4 Quoted in Janine Burke, *Field of Vision: A Decade of Change: Women's Art in the Seventies* (Ringwood, Vic.: Penguin Books, 1990), p.36.

In Cotton's darkroom solitude is assured. 'It was wonderful', she recalled, first having a darkroom of her own, 'and nobody else coming in and out and having to use some of the apparatus'.[5] A darkroom at home, although sometimes considered, was never desired:

> *When you're home other things are on your mind and you think you'd better stop for a minute and there's something you should go and do, or what am I going to make for tea tonight?*[6]

Though it does not aim to do so, Olive Cotton's photography speaks about the worth of such intangibles as time, solitude and effort. It also gently makes a claim for the value of what could be called the private or 'other' sphere invariably inhabited by women artists in the years following the Second World War when many of the hard-won professional and social gains of the preceding decades were lost. There have been long periods in which Cotton's photography has been invisible to the object-oriented eyes of art and/or photographic history. Because it has had no public presence it has therefore been assumed not to exist, a situation with numerous parallels in other areas of women's activities such as diary writing.[7]

> *The women artists of this period* [the 1920s and 1930s] *are not some isolated out-crop of female talent but the culmination of forty years of growing feminist awareness and increasing liberty for women.*[8]

White women had gained the vote Australia-wide by 1908 and had begun to reap the benefits of the expanded educational and employment opportunities that flowed from the social and political radicalism of the 1880s and 1890s. Born in 1911, Olive Edith Cotton belonged to a generation of women for whom a whole range of new possibilities existed, 'in image, life-style and career'.[9]

---

5 *Light Years*, op. cit.
6 Ibid.
7 Women's diaries are now often claimed as 'a form of literary self-representation' that challenges 'masculinist standards of autobiography and literature generally'. See Katie Holmes, "'Diamonds of the Dustheap"? Women's Diary Writing between the Wars' in Maryanne Dever (ed.), *Wallflowers and Witches: Women and Culture in Australia 1910–1945* (St Lucia, Qld: University of Queensland Press, 1994), p.39. Other areas of previously undervalued activity include the compilation of photographic albums; see Isobel Crombie, 'Private Lives: The Work and Life of Viscountess Frances Jocelyn' (MA Prelim., University of Melbourne, 1993).
8 Janine Burke, *Australian Women Artists 1840–1940* (Collingwood, Vic.: Greenhouse, 1980), p.41.
9 Ibid., p.39.

Cotton's home environment was stimulating and supportive. From the outset, a love of nature and of the arts was intertwined, a reflection of her parents' interests. Her mother, Florence (nee Channon), had studied painting under Datillo Rubbo; she was an accomplished china painter and based her designs on botanical drawings. Music was also an integral part of family life. Cotton's mother played the piano and encouraged both of her daughters to learn music. Cotton studied piano privately until age eighteen, competing publicly in eisteddfods until the early 1930s. Her father, Leo Cotton, was a geologist with an interest in amateur photography; he took photographs on Sir Ernest Shackleton's expedition to Antarctica in 1907. Another great influence was her free-thinking grandfather, Frank Cotton, an MP in the first Labor caucus. He was vitally concerned with social issues and closely followed the social and economic progress in the newly created Union of Soviet Socialist Republics (USSR).

The eldest of five children, Cotton grew up on the family's large block at Hornsby on Sydney's north shore; their twenty acres of natural bushland tumbled down a hillside into a valley, a haven for a young child free to wander at her will.[10] Cousins who lived on an adjacent property were frequent playmates.

The beginning of her lifelong passion for photography came at the age of eleven when an aunt gave her a Kodak No.0 Box Brownie camera. When she started using the camera she sensed 'a great awakening', having discovered photography as an ideal means of self-expression. Her father encouraged her new interest and taught her film processing and printing in a darkroom he set up in 'the laundry ... with the enlarger plugged into the ironing light'.[11]

Cotton used to take photographs wherever she could—around her home, in the garden and in the bush. A camera always accompanied her on annual family holidays to Newport on the New South Wales coast where she and family friend, Max Dupain, would 'roam all around Newport together taking pictures'.[12] Newport, later described by Dupain as 'a weekender's paradise, a peaceful escape from city life',[13] provided numerous photographic opportunities: the atmospheric *She-oaks* was taken at Bungan Head; the small figure in the right-hand side of the composition is Dupain.

---

10 After her mother's death, Cotton's father gave approximately thirty acres of adjacent bushland to the Hornsby Shire Council to be preserved as the Florence Cotton Memorial Park.

11 Interview with Olive Cotton, 'Australian Women Photographers Research Project', 1981, National Gallery of Australia registry file 81/842.

12 Unsourced quotes are from Olive Cotton's captions to the photographs in this book.

13 Max Dupain, *Max Dupain's Australian Landscapes* (Ringwood, Vic.: Viking, 1988), p.103.

From 1921 to 1929, Cotton attended the Methodist Ladies' College in Burwood; in her final year, she was head prefect and won an award which covered her university fees. Also in 1929, at the age of eighteen, she joined the Photographic Society of New South Wales (which had begun to admit women members only seven years earlier). It was an indication of the seriousness of her intentions and of the desire to improve her photographic skills. She later recalled:

> [Harold] *Cazneaux,* [Cecil] *Bostock, Bill Buckle, all those wonderful people were there. You'd take photographs along and they would be criticised. What made it a terrific experience was that you tried so hard each time to have something worthwhile.*[14]

Cotton was one of the growing number of women to whom a university education was available. She attended Sydney University from 1930 to 1934, graduating with a Bachelor of Arts and majors in English and mathematics. Other subjects studied included psychology, botany and geology.

Following her graduation she decided against teaching, for which her father had advocated, and which was the usual choice for women of her background. Instead, she wanted to pursue a career in photography, and in mid-1934 went to work in Max Dupain's studio at 24 Bond Street, Sydney. Dupain had established his business the previous year after completing a three-year stint in the studio of Cecil Bostock. The timing was fortunate as Australia was slowly recovering from the ravages of the Great Depression and business opportunities were beginning to expand, especially in the field of photographic illustration (now known as professional or commercial photography, encompassing fashion and advertising work).

Olive Cotton and Max Dupain worked together for more than six years; the partnership ending in early 1941 with the break-up of their two-year-old marriage, and Cotton's departure for Mittagong, New South Wales, to teach mathematics at Frensham School.

It was during the days in the Bond Street studio that both photographers consolidated their skills and began to develop their distinctive visions. But the nature of their involvement in the then predominant spheres of photographic activity—photographic illustration and exhibition photography (now generally termed 'art photography')—was quite different. For a complex mix

14 From an interview with Olive Cotton in 1981, quoted in Barbara Hall and Jenni Mather, *Australian Women Photographers 1840–1960* (Melbourne: Greenhouse, 1986), p.83. One of Cotton's photographs was published in the Methodist Ladies' College magazine, *The Excelsior,* in 1928.

of personal and social factors Cotton became established in only one sphere; Dupain on the other hand became ensconced in both.

Cotton's first exhibited photograph was *Dusk*, which was shown at the New South Wales Photographic Society's Interstate Exhibition in 1932. By the late 1930s, Cotton was a regular participant in exhibitions organised by the photographic societies. In 1937, *Shasta daisies* and *Quartet* (now called *The Budapest String Quartet)* were selected for the Victorian Salon of Photography's exhibition *International Camera Pictures*. The catalogue noted that such exhibitions were held throughout the world by like-minded groups:

> *in very large part, they are hobby Exhibitions, not for the hope of gain, not for the hope of glory; but for beauty itself and for the interchange of ideas amongst kindred spirits.*[15]

Cotton also sent photographs to England where they were hung in photography salons. *Teacup ballet* was included in the London Salon of Photography exhibition in 1935; two years later, *Shasta daisies* and *Winter willows* were shown at the same venue. *Winter willows* was reproduced in the British publication *The Penrose Annual* in 1938 where the author praised its artistic value: 'the possibilities of so very complex a tangle of movements, rhythms, and spacing shown in *Winter willows'* were regarded as evidence of keen perception, 'recorded aptly with no hint of "artiness"'.[16]

Dupain's exhibition photography, too, had attracted considerable attention, for example, in the exhibitions mounted by the Photographic Society of New South Wales in the early 1930s. But it was his work as a photographic illustrator that had the greatest effect on the Sydney scene. His 'fine still life, figure and portrait work'[17] was particularly admired, and his bold, innovative style was sought after by a variety of prestigious clients including the Australian Broadcasting Commission and David Jones. Within just a year or two of the opening of his studio, Max Dupain's name was everywhere, especially in the pages of Sydney Ure Smith's influential magazines *The Home* and *Art in Australia*.

It was not until the outbreak of the Second World War and Dupain's subsequent enlistment that Cotton fully entered the professional sphere. Until that time, the delineation between her and

---

15 Introduction to the *Catalogue of International Camera Pictures* exhibited in The Athenaeum Gallery, Melbourne, 18 to 30 October 1937 (Melbourne: Victorian Salon of Photography, 1937).
16 Jan Gordon, 'Art in Photography', *The Penrose Annual: Review of the Graphic Arts*, 1938, vol.40, p.27.
17 Gael Newton (ed.), *Max Dupain* (Sydney: David Ell Press, 1980), p.24.

Dupain's respective positions was clear. She had joined the Max Dupain Studio not as a partner but as an assistant. Her duties included making appointments, attending to models, assisting with processing Dupain's negatives and prints, and spotting his prints. In contrast to Geoff Powell and Damien Parer, who joined the studio in the late 1930s, Cotton did not work as a photographer.[18]

She had no delusions about her role or her comparative lack of visibility at the time. With regard to her *Fashion shot, Cronulla sandhills* showing a model being photographed by Dupain, she later commented:

> *The model was Noreen Hallard and Max was taking fashion shots for David Jones in the sandhills ... I was just the general dogs-body assistant taking shots to please myself.*[19]

Girl with mirror was taken under similar circumstances: the model was awaiting 'her turn to be photographed by Max, whose camera tripod casts the ... lines of shadow in the top left-hand corner'.

Retrospectively, too, Cotton has been rendered invisible by writers like Niall Brennan, one of Damien Parer's biographers. He eulogises the Max Dupain Studio as an all-male environment, in which big issues like religion were frequently discussed: 'The men of the studio talked and argued, sometimes heatedly, over their lunchtime pies and cups of tea'.[20]

The imbalance in Cotton's and Dupain's professional standing was quite typical of the period. Very few women photographers ran their own studios between the wars[21]; they were far more likely to work as assistants to male photographers, sometimes members of their families. In Sydney, for instance, the Cazneaux daughters worked tirelessly for their father Harold Cazneaux, while in Melbourne, Athol Shmith's sister Verna helped run his studio. International photographic history is also replete with the stories of unequal husband and wife partnerships, Lucia Moholy's cryptically titled book *Marginal Notes*[22] being just one account of a working relationship with a far more famous husband (Laszlo Moholy-Nagy).

---

18 For further information on Powell, see Helen Ennis, 'Searching for Geoffrey Powell' in Stuart Koop (ed.), *Shot* (Fitzroy, Vic.: Centre for Contemporary Photography, 1992), pp.37–45.

19 Quoted in 'Coming Events/Special Interest', *Graphics Monthly*, August 1986.

20 Niall Brennan, *Damien Parer: Cameraman* (Carlton, Vic.: Melbourne University Press, 1994), p.64.

21 Hall and Mather (op. cit., p.83) have noted that very few women served as 'role models' for Cotton: 'May Moore's name was a fading legend (in the early thirties the studio was being run by a male photographer, under the original name)' and recollections of photographers such as Bernice Agar, Judith Fletcher and Florence Milson were very faint. The two women photographers whose work particularly impressed Cotton were Margaret Michaelis and Olga Sharp.

22 Lucia Moholy, *Marginalien zu Moholy-Nagy: Marginal Notes* (Krefeld: Scherpe, 1972).

And yet there was obviously a fertile exchange of ideas between Dupain and Cotton, whose shared love of photography dated from their teenage years. They worked together closely, sometimes photographing the same subjects (for example, the Budapest String Quartet and Jean Lorraine). Dupain is the crouching figure in *Among the beeches* taking his own photograph of the scene. They also helped each other by occasionally posing as models. Dupain's *Portrait of Olive Cotton* taken at the beach in 1935 is a striking modernist composition. Her *Max after surfing* (1937), though taken indoors, is equally dramatic—torso sensuously illuminated and striking face in shadow.[23] *Max Dupain,* Cotton's portrait of the laughing Dupain taken on the doorstep of their home at Longueville, is intimate and delightfully informal.

Not surprisingly, in view of the gender and professional inequalities, it has generally been assumed that Cotton was influenced by Dupain—he has been described as her 'mentor'[24]—and not vice versa. But, like numerous other strong-minded women in similar situations, Cotton developed her own ways of working that ensured her independence. In an interview in 1981, she provided an insight into their relationship: 'When I was climbing up on stools using the studio camera to take *Shasta daisies,* Max thought I was wasting my time, but anyway, it turned out quite well'. She did not like anyone giving her advice 'because you feel that you've considered everything before you present the final print, it's your idea. [If] anybody else wants to impose their ideas, I don't like it'.[25]

After-hours, Cotton worked on her exhibition photography, making the most of the studio facilities and equipment. She used Dupain's wonderful Thornton Pickard studio camera that took 6 × 8 inch negatives[26] in addition to her own Rolleiflex camera purchased in 1937. She later recalled:

> *It was nice in the studio in Sydney, you could do all sorts of things. It was a very big space and Max had a large ground glass screen made in two or three pieces but it was very high, it was like another wall and you could slide it across on runners and ... you could put lights behind it and you could get this diffused lighting, back lighting and all sorts of things.*[27]

---

23 Only one known vintage print of *Max after surfing* exists and it has never been exhibited.
24 Michael Richardson, 'A Therapeutic Calm', *Australian Photography*, September 1991, vol.42, no.9, p.4.
25 Hall and Mather, op. cit., p.84.
26 The camera was given to Dupain by his father 'as a starting off present ... a beautiful, handmade timber camera with double dark slides made for housing glass plates ... It weighed a ton': Dupain, op. cit., p.8.
27 Interview with Olive Cotton, 'Australian Women Photographers Research Project'.

The studio also provided a stimulating environment that was constantly nourished by visitors—models, clients, other photographers and artists. Among those who became close friends were Olga Sharp, model Jean Lorraine, the artists Douglas Annand and Richard Beck, and Geoff Powell and Damien Parer.

According to Neil McDonald, another Parer biographer, Parer was 'equally fond' of Dupain and Cotton; McDonald, however, went on to describe Cotton in somewhat patronising terms as:

> *a quiet, soft-spoken girl whose rather self-effacing manner concealed a brilliant mind and considerable creative ability.*[28]

Cotton considered Parer to be 'like a ... member of the family'.[29] Studio life was informal, interruptions were not an issue and models would drop in for coffee and conversation. Everyone from the studio would go with Dupain on his fashion shoots to Bungart Beach near Newport, an ideal spot for out-of-doors fashion work. Cotton's snapshot of Damien Parer and Phyl Riley (the model in *Beachwear fashion shot)* jumping off the sandhills captures the light-hearted spirit of these days. When the Cotton/Dupain relationship ended in 1941, Damien Parer wrote to Dupain:

> *I was bloody sorry about you and Olive having a bust up—the combination was such a cracker one—and I like you both so much—I feel it can't be permanent—don't think I am an interfering bastard when I say that.*[30]

But it was permanent. Cotton moved to Mittagong where she taught mathematics for two terms at Frensham School, prompting the newspaper headline, 'Wife Prefers Mathematics to Marriage!'.[31] However, with the deepening of the war crisis, she was keen to contribute in some way to the war effort. This became possible in late 1941 when Ernest Hyde and Max Dupain invited her to return to Sydney to manage the Dupain Studio while Dupain served as a camouflage officer in the RAAF. A few months earlier, the studio had moved to 49 Clarence Street, amalgamating with Hartland & Hyde—the pre-eminent process engravers in Australia at the time and leaders in the introduction of colour photography to Sydney.[32]

---

28 Neil McDonald, *War Cameraman: The Story of Damien Parer* (Port Melbourne, Vic.: Lothian, 1994), p.24.
29 Ibid., p.25.
30 Ibid., p.120.
31 *Daily Telegraph*, 21 February 1943, p.19.
32 Max Dupain, op. cit., p.15. Two floors of the building were devoted to Hartland & Hyde's activities, while the Max Dupain Studio occupied another floor. On occasion, the Dupain Studio would work for Hartland & Hyde.

Cotton accepted the invitation and the challenge:

> *I thought, Oh well I'll be on my own, so I went back ... which was really nice because I could do all the practical work and I didn't have to worry about the accounts. Hartland & Hyde looked after that part of it ... I had my little reception room [that] also housed their switch girl and switchboard for the whole set up and she was my receptionist too.*[33]

Women's participation in the Australian workforce increased significantly during wartime, rising from 664,000 in 1939 to 855,000 in 1944; this was, however, seen as a temporary phenomenon, for the duration of the war only.[34] Olive Cotton was just one of the thousands of women who relished the greatly enhanced employment opportunities. She managed the Max Dupain Studio from 1942 to 1945, a period which she later described as 'really great years'.[35] Now, for the first time, she could practise as a professional photographer, her stamp reading 'Olive Cotton, Max Dupain Studios'. Her entry into the professional sphere was marked by a dramatic expansion in her repertoire; the portraiture, landscapes and still lives that had been predominant in her exhibition photography of the 1930s were augmented by views of Sydney, interiors and various commissions related to war propaganda. *Aircraft mechanics,* for example, was one of the photographs she was commissioned to take for a book on the RAAF, *Wings of Tomorrow*.[36]

Studio portraiture remained a key area of activity as the opportunities for advertising illustration decreased in the war years. Nevertheless, publications played a vital role in disseminating Cotton's work to a broad audience; her photographs were published in Sydney Ure Smith's wartime magazine *Australia National Journal* and in *Bank Notes,* a magazine issued by the Commonwealth Bank of Australia which gave a high profile to photography.[37]

The most ambitious commission at the time was a photographic mural of a ballet scene produced for a client of Sydney architect Samuel Lipson in 1942. Photographic murals had come into vogue following the success of Russell Roberts's impressive mural installation at

33 Interview with Olive Cotton, 'Australian Women Photographers Research Project'.

34 Prime Minister John Curtin stated that 'he would prevent the erosion of men's jobs by the encroachment of "cheap female labour"; and that all women who occupied traditionally "men's jobs" would be replaced as soon as possible': Anne Summers, *Damned Whores and God's Police: The Colonization of Women in Australia* (Ringwood, Vic.: Penguin, 1975), p.414.

35 Quoted in Hall and Mather, op. cit., p.85.

36 Clive Turnbull, *Wings of Tomorrow,* with illustrations by Roderick M. Shaw (Sydney: F.H. Johnston, 1945).

37 Hartland & Hyde used one of Cotton's portraits in an advertisement in *Australia National Journal*'s September 1943 issue. One of Cotton's photographs was published in Peter Bellew (ed.), *Pioneering Ballet in Australia* (Sydney: Craftsman Bookshop, 1945).

the Australian pavilion at the New York World Fair in 1939 (the installation was designed by Cotton's friend Douglas Annand). Evidence suggests, however, that Lipson's commitment to photography was greater than that of his client who greeted Cotton's request for payment with 'What! Nineteen pounds just for a big photograph!'[38] The production of *Theme for a mural* was complex and time-consuming, involving more than one hundred hours work' and an all-night effort processing the print.

In October 1945, Cotton—using her married name of McInerney—worked on what proved to be one of her most significant projects. It was a series of photographs for a book on Sturt, a progressive school that had opened in Mittagong, New South Wales, in October 1941, not far from Frensham where she had earlier taught mathematics. The school had been established by Frensham's founder, Winifred West, an ardent and creative educationalist; it grew quickly and by 1945 had a weekly attendance of around 150 students.

Eleven years earlier, West had commissioned Harold Cazneaux to take the photographs for *The Frensham Book*, which depicted life at the girls' boarding school.[39] In the *Sturt* book, too, West conceived a key role for photography. Early in 1946, she wrote to a friend:

> *There will be about 50 photographs divided into sections: The Garden; The House; Spinning; Dyeing; Weaving; Flowers; Carpenters; Other People; Children's Library & we are now trying to find suitable quotations to put at the beginning of each section.*[40]

Despite the difficulties posed by the endemic shortage of supplies during wartime, the book was published by Olga Sharp in October 1946. It was, in Winifred West's words, a testament to the school as 'a happy meeting place for people young and old who love beauty and good craftsmanship'.[41] Especially memorable are Cotton's evocative photographs of Sturt's garden, her finely observed close-ups of flowers and unobtrusive studies of children absorbed in their activities.[42]

38 From a conversation with Olive Cotton and Helen Ennis quoted in the author's entry on Cotton in Joan Kerr (ed.), *Heritage: The National Women's Art Book* (Sydney: Art and Australia, 1995), p.132.

39 *The Frensham Book: 100 Pictures by Cazneaux of an Australian school* (Sydney: Art in Australia, 1934).

40 Winifred West to Kathleen Hassell 1946, quoted in Priscilla Kennedy, *Portrait of Winifred West* (Gordon, NSW: Fine Arts Press, 1976), p.149.

41 Winifred West, 'Introduction' in Olive Cotton, *Sturt* (Wahroonga, NSW: Olga Sharp for Winifred West, 1946).

42 The book also contained two photographs by Olga Sharp, whom Cotton had met when Sharp worked in the advertising department of AWA. Sharp was 'also a clever artist and a sculptress', who later had a photographic studio at Wahroonga where she used to photograph children: 'some of her work was very sensitive and she had a lovely feeling for it': Interview with Olive Cotton, 'Australian Women Photographers Research Project'.

Cotton also contributed eleven photographs to Helen Blaxland's *Flower Pieces* published in 1946 on the art of flower arrangements; Max Dupain was the other principal photographer. It was one of the few occasions where their photographs were published together and, even within the strict confines of the commission, the differences in approach and emphasis are unmistakable. Cotton's studies of flower arrangements in domestic interiors are light-filled and airy, while Dupain makes use of theatrical lighting and strong shadows.[43]

It was one of the last public appearances of Olive Cotton's photographs for nearly four decades. With the end of the war and Dupain's return from service, Cotton's tenure in the studio was over. In 1946, Cotton and Ross Mclnerney moved to the Cowra district, where the Mclnerneys had farmed for nearly eighty years.

> *the distinction conventionally applied to the art of the inter-war period—that is, between 'the traditional' and 'the modern'—is ... at best relative; certainly it was not perceived in the categorical form which has subsequently been projected onto the period.*[44]

In Australian photographic history, the 1930s are characterised by the demise of Pictorialism (a movement known colloquially as 'the fuzzy wuzzy school' that had been dominant in photography circles since the early 1900s) and the rise of modernism. Pictorialist work is invariably devalued in this scenario, considered to be out-of-step with the realities of modern life. The beauty of the new age, wrote G.H. Saxon Mills in 1931, 'is only for those who themselves are aware of the "zeitgest" who belong consciously and proudly to this age, and have not their eyes forever wistfully fixed on the past'.[45]

Olive Cotton's photography has generally been viewed within a modernist context, her photographs being read as further evidence in the anti-Pictorialism, pro-modernism case. Consequently, it is her work from the late 1930s that has been of principal interest for it coincides with the final stages of the alleged battle between oppositional reactionary and progressive forces. But, as artist and writer Ian Burn has noted, the predominance of modernist views in the writing

43 Helen Blaxland thanked the photographers 'for all the time, patience, and unfailing good humour they have expended on these photographs, and for the high standard of technical excellence they have attained': Helen Blaxland, *Flower Pieces* (Sydney: Ure Smith, 1946), p.8. The blocks for the book were engraved by Hartland & Hyde.

44 Ian Burn, *National Life and Landscapes: Australian Painting 1900–1940*(Sydney: Bay Books, 1990), p.10.

45 Max Dupain read this essay in 1931 and claimed it to be influential in the development of his own ideas; see Helen Ennis, *Max Dupain: A Portrait* (Sydney: Fourth Estate, 2024).

about art misrepresents the historical situation by ignoring 'the more traditional work'.[46] Cotton's photography offers a richer glimpse of the period providing an alternative to the pervasive either/or dialectic, and inviting a reconsideration of both Pictorialism and modernism. In her work, there is not simply an overlap between the two allegedly contradictory styles and attitudes, but also an interchange between them that underpins her entire photographic career.

Modernism came later to photography in Australia than to the other visual arts; by the 1920s, its appearance in painting, printmaking and postermaking was commonplace. However, it was not until the early 1930s that modernist photographs began to be regularly exhibited and published.[47]

The rhetoric associated with modernism was often highly charged, espousing the birth of a new era and the wonders of contemporary life. Dupain was one of its most forceful advocates. Outraged by the conservatism and smugness of the *Commemorative Salon of Photography,* a large exhibition organised by various photographic societies as part of Australia's 150th anniversary celebrations, he passionately declared:

> *Great art has always been contemporary in spirit. To-day we feel the surge of aesthetic exploration along abstract lines, the social economic order impinging itself on art, the repudiation of the 'truth to nature criterion', and the galvanising of art and psychology.*[48]

Rather than reflecting 'the elements of modern adventure and research', the collection of photographs on display was 'a flaccid thing, a gentle narcotic, something to soothe our tired nerves after a weary day at the office!'[49]

Soon after the *Commemorative Salon,* a small group of Sydney photographers and designers established the Contemporary Camera Groupe, its name marking an apparent break with the past. But the group's membership indicated that the battle lines between traditional and modernist 'factions' were not as clearly drawn as has since been assumed. Members who participated in the exhibition held at the David Jones' Gallery in Sydney in November 1938 included older-generation Pictorialists—Cecil Bostock, William Buckle and Harold Cazneaux—as well as

---

46 Burn, *National Life and Landscapes*, p.10.
47 Harold Cazneaux's work for *The Home* magazine in the late 1920s is often taken as a precedent.
48 Max Dupain, 'Arc of the Camera' [Letter to the editor], *Sydney Morning Herald*, 30 March 1938. The exhibition was held at the Commonwealth Bank Chambers, Sydney, from 25 March to 9 April 1938; Cotton was represented with four works.
49 Ibid.

new-wave modernists—Max Dupain, Laurence Le Guay, Damien Parer and Russell Roberts. The other participants were graphic designers Douglas Annand, A.E. Dodd and Louis Witts. Olive Cotton (the only female member) was represented with eleven works.[50]

Like some of her colleagues, Cotton contributed to both the *Commemorative Salon* and the Camera Groupe's *Exhibition of Photographic Studies*. She did not declare her allegiance to Pictorialism or modernism at the time, nor has she seen the need to do so since. Her published statements on her own photographic practice or photography generally are very few; when she has spoken, it has been in a conversational, rather than polemical mode. Nevertheless, her position has been clear. Since the mid-1930s to the present day, she has produced both Pictorialist and modernist photographs without privileging one style over another.

Her earliest photographs such as *She-oaks* and *Dusk* accord with Pictorialist criteria; they are soft-focus, generalised landscapes that are moody in atmosphere. *Storm,* with bare, dark trees silhouetted against a stormy sky, is an equally timeless and placeless image. Cotton, however, never used the full range of Pictorialist devices—eschewing, for instance, the bromoil process and other printing techniques advocated by Cazneaux and other prominent Pictorialists.

From the mid-1930s, Cotton began experimenting with a variety of approaches in both her studio and outdoor work. She introduced different vantage points, more extreme angles and increasingly abstract compositions, all of which are associated with modernist photography (also known as the New Photography). *Grass at sundown, Papyrus, Willow rain, Escape* and *Fire escape* are examples of the 'up-shots' or 'worm's eye' views made infamous by modernist photographers in Europe and the United States in the 1920s. The low vantage point Cotton adopts in *Beachwear fashion shot* creates a striking composition calculated to draw the viewer's attention to the bathing suit. Lens flare is embraced as a surprising compositional element in *Grass at sundown* and *Willow rain.*

In the studio, she continued her experimentation, carefully setting up still lives such as *Teacup ballet, Plum blossom* and *Shasta daisies,* and photographing them under tightly controlled lighting conditions. More overt forms of manipulation included using multiple negatives to produce a

50 The introduction to the catalogue outlined the Groupe's aims: 'We have built this little unit in order to strengthen the liaison between photography and the other arts. We hate the cliche, and would drive a wedge between stagnant orthodoxy and original thought of the living moment. At the same time, we do not take this step in the dark without reference to our masters whom we love': *Exhibition of Photographic Studies by Contemporary Camera Groupe* (Sydney: David Jones' Exhibition Gallery, 1938).

print: *Windflowers* and *Sky submerged* were created from two negatives, while *Theme for a mural* emerged from a combination of negatives and prints.

Cotton belonged to a circle of photographers who were well informed about overseas trends, largely through publications—especially the German annual *Das Deutsche Lichtbild* (The German Photograph) and the English annual *Modern Photography*. The Australian magazine *Australasian Photo-Review* also carried reports on recent developments overseas. Dupain's description of the Bond Street studio days proffers a dizzying array of influences and unforgettable events:

> *such as the rediscovery of solarisation; the portraits of famous conductors and musicians* ... [for] *the ABC; the new flexibilities of double printing; the discovery of Man Ray and the radical thinking of his Dada confederates; the sheer professionalism of Edward Steichen; the new work being done overseas and its arrival on our doorstep in magazine form.*[51]

These were, he concluded, 'shared by the interesting people I had around me including my first wife Olive ... Geoff Powell ... [and] Damien Parer'.[52]

Specific influences on Cotton's photography are harder to pinpoint as she has spoken very little of them. She refutes the belief that Surrealism was a factor in the production of *Theme for a mural*, as has sometimes been claimed. The techniques used were simply 'the means to an end'; most important was the creation of a picture in which 'the different elements held together as one scene'.[53]

Cotton's version of modernism was always somewhat idiosyncratic, never strictly following a modernist agenda. In the USSR and Germany—the birthplaces of modernist photography—the correlation between modern photography and urban industrial life was emphasised. As Russian artist Alexander Rodchenko saw it in 1928:

> *Modern cities with their many-storey buildings, special factory installations, display windows reaching to a height of two or three storeys, trams, motor cars, luminous advertisements and neon signs, steamers, aeroplanes ... all this has necessarily changed the customary psyche of visual perception. It is as though only the camera were able to depict life as it is today.*[54]

---

51 Max Dupain, op. cit., p.12.
52 Ibid.
53 From conversations between Olive Cotton and Helen Ennis; see entry in Kerr, *Heritage*, p.132.
54 Alexander Rodchenko, 'Ways of Contemporary Photography', *Novyj LEF*, 1928, no.9, pp.31–39; quoted in Herbert Molderings, 'Urbanism and Technological Utopianism. Thoughts on the Photography of Neue Sachlichkeit and the Bauhaus' in David Mellor (ed.), *Germany: The New Photography 1927–33* (London: Arts Council of Great Britain, 1978), p.91.

In Australia, too, it was the identification with urban industrial life and all its trappings that was taken to signify modernity. (Locally, modernity referred simply to modern life; it was not linked, as in the USSR, to the building of a utopian socialist state.) Cotton, however, was not one of those who devoted themselves exclusively to photographing modern subject matter. Images of the city or of city-life appear infrequently in her work, mainly being confined to the small group of architectural views of Sydney taken during the war years. *City rooftops* and *Darling Harbour,* both taken from the windows of the Clarence Street studio in 1942 are two fine examples.

The only time she used modern, everyday objects in a still life was in *Teacup ballet.* Now Cotton's best known image, it has been celebrated as a modernist icon, often being erroneously described as an advertisement for china.[55] To a contemporary viewer, the cups may well function as emblems of modernity—just like the domestic objects in Margaret Preston's still life paintings of the 1920s—but to Cotton they offered the possibility of making 'a photograph to express a dance theme'.

Like *Teacup ballet, Glasses,* which was commissioned as an advertisement for spectacle frames, relies for its impact on the dramatic effects of studio lighting. The composition is one of Cotton's most spare: all detail has been eliminated to ensure that the glasses and their distorted shadows are the key players.

Even in what could be described as Cotton's most experimental period—the years 1935 to 1945—naturalistic views went hand-in-hand with the more extreme vantage points, depending on the subject matter being photographed and the effect desired. The three figures in *Aircraft mechanics,* for example, are photographed straight-on without recourse to the heroism of the wartime photography of Edward Cranstone and others.[56] Men and machine are linked together in a composition filled with curves and circular forms. It is the organic, workaday relationship between them that is given expression.

55 See, for example, Gael Newton, *Shades of Light: Photography and Australia 1839–1988* (Canberra: Australian National Gallery, 1988), p.119; and Alan McCulloch and Susan McCulloch, *Encyclopaedia of Australian Art,* 2nd edn. (St Leonards, NSW: Allen & Unwin, 1994), p.182.

56 See, for example, Edward Cranstone's photographs for the Department of Information and the Allied Works Council in the collection of the National Gallery of Australia. Cranstone gave the male figure iconic status; his 'precisely evocative images of strength and heroism [were] constructed around strong diagonal compositions and severe upward looking camera angles': Martyn Jolly, 'Edward Cranstone, Photographer', *Photofile,* Autumn 1984, p.2. See also, Laurence Le Guay's immediate post-war photography, examples of which are illustrated in his article 'Photomontage', *Contemporary Photography,* March–April 1947, vol.1, no.3, pp.24–27.

The holistic point of view developed by Cotton often seems at odds with the desire for tension, drama and dominance characteristic of much modernist photography. Hers is a democratic approach that treats all subjects equally, be they people, flowers or teacups. In her photographs of groups of people, such as *The Budapest String Quartet* and *Woolloomooloo Free Kindergarten*, no individual is emphasised at the expense of any other. Likewise, in the numerous flower studies taken over the decades, it is usually the group as a whole that is the focus of attention, not the individual flowers.

Cotton had no long-term interest in what could be called modernism's 'heroic vocabulary'. Very rarely did she monumentalise forms, making them larger than life. *The sleeper* epitomises the kind of harmony that was sought and that would reappear in *Children's garden* many years later. Olga Sharp is the sleeper in the bush; wildflower pinned to her blouse, she lies on her back in an unselfconscious, open pose. Beyond her in full sunshine are tall grasses and trees. Sharp is at peace with her environment, 'content in the bush setting which she loved'. Cotton approaches her quietly, tenderly, crouching down to assume an empathic vantage point.

As a figure in the landscape, *The sleeper* invites comparison with Max Dupain's iconic *Sunbaker* of c.1938. Here, a young man fresh out of the surf lies face-down on the sand, water droplets drying on him. His body is taut, ready to spring into action, his monumental form and angular limbs dominating his surroundings.

The contentment in nature expressed so beautifully in *The sleeper* is in fact a leitmotif of Cotton's photography. Her preferred subject matter has always been found well away from the hubbub of city life; aside from portraiture, it is the landscapes and studies of trees and flowers that are woven most tightly through more than six decades of photographic work. And it is in these photographs in particular that one sees the interplay between Pictorialism and modernism: the Pictorialist image *Storm* of 1935 is echoed in *Vapour trail* of 1991, while the modernist viewpoint seen in *Papyrus* in 1938 reappears in *Agapanthus* in 1955 and again in *Dead sunflowers* in 1984.[57] For Olive Cotton, the adoption of one approach has never involved a renunciation of the other.

57 Max Dupain has been one of the few to comment on the relevance of Pictorialism to Cotton's contemporary work. In his review of the retrospective exhibition *Olive Cotton—Photographs 1924–84* at the Australian Centre for Photography, Sydney, in 1985 he remarked, 'The influence of the Pictorial School is very apparent and even with her later work she remains faithful to her training and thinking in the Twenties and Thirties': Max Dupain, 'Olive Cotton: Works That Act as the Soul's Narcotic', *Sydney Morning Herald*, 16 October 1985.

> *all were plunged into the turmoil of the Second Great War, and now in its passing we are all struggling to reestablish the things that are worth living for.*[58]

When Olive McInerney moved to the Cowra district in 1946, both she and her photographic work slipped out of sight, out of the public sphere and into another, which involved marriage, motherhood and farm life. No longer could her activities be accounted for in the official languages associated with professional photography or with art and photographic history.

Indeed, only twice in the next thirty-five years did Olive Cotton's work speak publicly again, and then only briefly: one photograph was published in *Australian Photography 1947* and five photographs were included in the exhibition *Creative Vision* held at the Workshop Arts Centre in Willoughby, Sydney, in 1964.[59] There could be no talk about her latest photographs, their technical details, their subject matter and style, the influences that could be discerned in them, their manner of presentation. But, although the terms of engagement had shifted, photography continued to be a vital part of Cotton's life.

Olive and Ross McInerney's first home was a tent pitched on her father-in-law's land in the hills of the Illunie Range, forty-five kilometres south of Cowra. Eventually, in 1951, they moved to their own property, Spring Forest, near Koorawatha. Ross McInerney was not a conventional farmer. He inherited from his father a deep commitment to conservation.[60] Even now only a small proportion of their land is farmed; feed in the paddocks around the house is turned over to the birds rather than to stock. The remaining land is uncleared, forming a National Parks and Wildlife Service wildlife refuge that is one of the last stands of native bush on the plains of the central west of New South Wales.

At Spring Forest, Cotton's childhood and early adult years spent close to the native bush took on a new relevance. While she missed her friends, relatives and swimming in the sea, she loved the feeling of space and freedom in her new, often harsh physical environment. Once again she could study nature firsthand, taking her camera with her as she walked around the property. Watching

---

58 Harold Cazneaux, 'Landscape Photography' in Oswald L. Ziegler (ed.), *Australian Photography 1947* (Sydney: Ziegler Gotham Publications, 1947), p.15.

59 Cotton was represented in *Australian Photography 1947* with *Mary Yardley*, a portrait of a young girl, p.85. The photographs she contributed to *Creative Vision* were nos 140–144 in the catalogue: *Power house, Lily, Winter willows, The Budapest String Quartet* and *Radio telescope*.

60 Ross McInerney is a marvellous raconteur of country life. His stories provided the inspiration for his then son-in-law, Geoffrey Lehmann, to write *Ross' Poems* (Sydney: Angus & Robertson, 1978).

and waiting underpinned her photography—sometimes it was years before the circumstances, the subject or the sky were 'just right'. The dead sunflowers at the edge of the garden, for example, were left for some time 'until an interesting sky' provided 'a suitable background'. Similarly, the vapour trails that Cotton often watched criss-crossing the sky high above Spring Forest could not be made into a satisfactory picture in 'airy, empty sky'; eventually, in 1991, she took a photograph when the oldest part of the trail 'blown by the wind, had feathered out and this, together with a narrow foreground of trees, gave stability to the composition'.

Cotton draws her pictorial material from her own surroundings, from her own life. Her camera was with her while she watched her children, Sally and Peter, play. In *Children's garden*, 'a paradise garden where children could do as they pleased', garden and childhood are twinned as ideal states. The children are self-absorbed, shadows play across them, merging them with their picturesque setting. Cotton, as photographer, is equally unobtrusive.

Spring Forest offered a wealth of natural subject matter, Cotton's approach to it having much in common with that championed by Harold Cazneaux. In his essay for *Australian Photography 1947*, Cazneaux argued that pictorial landscape photography could still be a vital force in the traumatic post-war era. The 'new worker' must not become 'caught up in the new "speed up" of life, with all the new cults and ideas, and the so-called modern art movement'.[61] There was another more enduring alternative:

> *in our grand open spaces will still be found the beauty of sunshine and shadow, the waving grasses on the hillsides, the winding stream, the towering gum. Sincere art comes from the heart and mind, and we will find such inspiration in the work of yesterday even if we are all involved in this super progress of so-called modern life and art.*[62]

Cotton found beauty in nature's complex formal alphabet. She did not take broad sweeping views of the landscape or of farmland around Koorawatha; medium and long distance shots are few. Instead, she turned her camera towards trees and flowers. And behind them all is the sky, setting off their patterns and rhythms.

---

61 Cazneaux, 'Landscape Photography', p.17. Max Dupain and Hal Missingham also contributed essays to Ziegler's *Australian Photography 1947*.
62 Ibid.

In 1959, Cotton began teaching mathematics at Cowra High School, a job that she enjoyed but was not able to continue once a Diploma of Education became a mandatory teaching qualification. With the loss of this much-needed employment in 1963, she was forced to consider other options. A year later, she opened a photographic studio in Cowra, in an arcade off the main street. She 'took it all as it came'[63]—photographing children, debutantes, weddings and school groups. Much of the work was done in peoples' own homes and whenever possible under natural lighting conditions.

The opening of the studio signified Cotton's return to the professional sphere but the activities in which she was involved no longer had currency within the dominant discourses of the time. Professional photography had been transformed in the years after the Second World War; portraiture had lost its prestige while architectural and industrial photography and photojournalism were now the most highly valued fields, dominated by male photographers such as Dupain and David Moore in Sydney and Wolfgang Sievers in Melbourne.

Cotton's business made a reasonable income. But its principal joy was the darkroom where at the end of the day she could turn to some of the thousands of unprinted negatives that had amassed over the years. However, it was not until the early 1980s when she ceased taking on clients that she was able to print in earnest. The intersecting interests of art photography and feminism provided a further stimulus.

In 1980, *Teacup ballet* reappeared for the first time in more than forty years; it was a full-page illustration in Gael Newton's *Silver and Grey: Fifty Years of Australian Photography 1900–1950*. A year later, Cotton was represented in the ground-breaking travelling exhibition *Australian Women Photographers 1890–1950,* curated by Jenni Mather, Christine Gillespie and Barbara Hall. Their project was part of a wave of feminise research that aimed to redress the imbalances in Australian art history.

For Cotton, it meant a context in which her work could be recognised, though it was not necessarily of her choosing; her wish is to be considered as a photographer rather than as a woman photographer. In 1983, she was awarded an Australia Council Grant to make exhibition prints; sixty-six of these were presented in her first one-person exhibition, *Olive Cotton—Photographs 1924–84,* held at the Australian Centre for Photography in Sydney in 1985. In her

63 *Light Years,* op. cit.

catalogue introduction, Barbara Hall drew attention to a 'problem' lying right at the heart of Cotton's rediscovery—the contemporary predilection for her modernist photographs and the lack of a context, or language with which to consider the others:

> *One needs to appreciate the courage of an exhibition concept which will risk earlier and later work being seen as minor side panels to the middle career images of the thirties and forties.*[64]

Max Dupain, ironically, was one who engaged publicly with Cotton's recent photographs. In his capacity as photography reviewer for the *Sydney Morning Herald*, he drew attention to the threads linking her work of the past and present:

> *The therapeutic calm of this exhibition is its major attraction. It's like walking through the bush early in the morning and suddenly being surprised by the appearance of a tranquil lake; serenity is the soul's narcotic ... In all these pictures of land forms, of slender tracery, mysterious gorges and bright sunlit poplars there weaves a wholesome clannish thread of family consciousness.*[65]

Following its successful showing in Sydney, *Olive Cotton—Photographs 1924–84* toured to regional galleries in Victoria, New South Wales and Queensland during 1986. From then, Cotton's photographs became increasingly visible in exhibitions at public institutions and at commercial galleries.[66] National and state cultural institutions purchased her work and, in 1991, *Teacup ballet* was published on a stamp issued on 13 May to mark the 150th anniversary of photography in Australia. In honour of the occasion, an exhibition of Cotton's photographs was shown at the Cowra Civic Chambers. Also in 1991, *Light Years*, Kathryn Millard's documentary film on Cotton's life and work, was released. The significance of Cotton's contribution to Australian cultural life was publicly and formally recognised in 1993 with the Australia Council award of a Visual Arts/Craft Board's Emeritus Fellowship. In 1995, Cotton's work had a high profile in various exhibitions mounted to celebrate the twentieth anniversary of International Women's Year.[67]

---

64 Barbara Hall, 'Introduction', *Olive Cotton—Photographs 1924–84* (Sydney: Australian Centre for Photography, 1985).
65 Dupain, 'Olive Cotton: Works That Act as the Soul's Narcotic'.
66 She held a one-person exhibition at Australian Girls Own Gallery in Canberra from 13 March to 2 April 1992; see the catalogue of the exhibition, *Olive Cotton* (Kingston, ACT: Australian Girls Own Gallery, 1992).
67 For example, her photographs were included in exhibitions held at the National Gallery of Australia, the Art Gallery of New South Wales and the National Library of Australia. They were also featured in *Clarice Becket, Olive Cotton: In a Certain Light*, an exhibition at the Ivan Dougherty Gallery, Sydney.

Over the years Ross had been observing this tree's struggle to survive, and he eventually took me to see it. The tree had only a cluster of leaves left on its one remaining live branch, and here and there were the hollow remains of former branches, dead and broken. These hollows, however, were nesting places for birds, one of which flew out and went soaring amongst the clouds.

Now in her mid-eighties, Olive Cotton continues to take photographs at Spring Forest; *The soaring bird* is one of her most recent works. Her photography has never followed a straight line but creates its own patterns with gentle sweeps backwards and forwards and from side to side. Subjects and styles sometimes selected decades earlier are lovingly revisited. Art historical methodology—such as chronology and notions of artistic development—do not seem to help explain the photographs, either individually or cumulatively.

But there are common threads that tie together the photographs of the last sixty years—keen observation skills, a profound engagement with the subject and a love of light. The most memorable photographs carry the viewer away from the documentary imperative of here and now, and into another realm. Through photography, Olive Cotton has been able to express her overwhelmingly positive view of the world, one in which beauty and tranquillity have pride of place.

Taken when she was seventy-three years old, *Wild plum* can be read equally as a tribute to spring and as a homage to a particular plum tree. A tree, one suspects, that is known intimately and is much loved. Like Pierre Bonnard's tiny painting of an almond tree in blossom in the collection of the Georges Pompidou Centre in Paris, it is an exultant image of a marvellous commonplace—spring.

Life in the country

Sally McInerney

The reflection below was written in 1995 when this book was first published.

This is a brief account of the years after the war, when my brother and I were born and got to know our parents, Olive and Ross, and their surroundings. In retrospect, it seems a curious kind of life, which did not follow many easily identifiable rural Australian traditions. It was certainly quite different to the life Olive had led in the city.

Our first home was a tent in the Illunie Range, near Koorawatha in the central west of New South Wales. We always used to say that we lived in the bush, rather than in the country. The native forest around us seemed an endless reservoir of nature, like the sea to which our mother was so attached, and which she missed. We lived in the tent for three years, then for about a year leased a small, isolated house in the foothills. (It was here that Olive had her first brief break from us, her children: she went for an exhilarating half-hour flight in her brother-in-law's little Auster, taking aerial photographs in which the tiny house can be seen surrounded by dark masses of trees, with cleared farmland in the distance.)

In 1951, we moved to Spring Forest, the family's present farm beside the Illunie Range. Ross, a conservationist far ahead of his time, could not bear to destroy the native bush still growing on most of Spring Forest. He felt that humans were only transients on the land and so he never cleared it to sow large crops or to run as many livestock as the place might hold. Now the farm contains the only tract of near-original native bush left on the level country in the central west of New South Wales; it flows from Spring Forest up into the Illunie hills, maintaining the old connections.

Ross's father, whose own father came to the district from Ireland empty-handed in the 1860s and unaccountably prospered, had lost most of his farmland in the 1930s depression. (Ross was born in 1918. Aged fourteen, he was taken on a long walk through the bush by an old family friend who kindly pointed out some bees' nests in near-inaccessible trees and said, 'There you are, young fellow, there's a start in life for you'. This was serious counsel, given to a boy who'd clearly have to start from scratch.) By 1939, the family had retreated from a solid house amongst rolling paddocks to their remaining mountain fastness deep in the Illunie Range. Here, the three oldest sons, John, Ross and Bryce, built a hut for their family from slabs of stringybark, rolled out and flattened to make panels for walls and roof; and then they went away to the war.

This family encampment, in a clearing shaded by stringybark saplings, was the place Olive came to with her new husband when the war was over. Our tent was pitched near the hut. Sunlight shone through a hole at the top of the roof-pole; my brother, Peter, my first and oldest friend, slept in a big cane pram. We went over to the hut for cooking and conviviality, and often returned to visit long after we'd moved away. There was no electricity, no telephone, no running water; Cowra, the nearest town, was about forty-five kilometres away over rough dirt roads. The three brothers had come back with no visible wounds from the war, though it had taken them to terrible places; to a child they seemed immensely tall, mercurial men who had fought an enormous bushfire somewhere; the fire was beaten, but still smouldering.

John (the first of the McInerneys ever to go to university) was a doctor who flew planes in Papua New Guinea after the war, but times were tough for young men coming back to farming life with no farmland of their own. I see now that the war still pervaded everything, and still feel safest, as perhaps our father and his brothers did, amongst the light-leaved, airy trees of the dry inland. Military relics lay around, put to use in various ways; horses wore Light Horse headstalls, army overcoats were extra blankets on the beds. Everything had to be done by hand with basic or improvised materials; work was incessant for both men and women. Clothes were washed out-of-doors in a copper boiling over an open fire; sheep had to be butchered for household meat; old pieces of machinery were constantly being repaired. Anything might be useful; nothing was wasted. (When, in 1979, the bank almost foreclosed on Spring Forest, it was stopped in the nick of time by the sale of a steam engine so old it had become antique.)

My brother and I played with the marvellous basic materials of nature. Ducklings, pups and kangaroo joeys were sometimes our companions. Peacocks wandered amongst the gum trees, safe from the chained-up dogs, and gave their eerie semi-human yells from the roof of the stringybark hut at night; their fallen tail-feathers, our playthings, stood in our grandmother's vases in lieu of flowers. There was much talking by the fire at night. Ross's father was a quiet-voiced man who would sometimes, with delicate sarcasm, ask wide-eyed city visitors what they thought of the Arcadian simplicity of the rural folk (though he never said that to Olive). Ross's mother (once a city girl from Glebe, in Sydney) was a great raconteur, like most of her family; it was wonderful to hear the pattern of talk and laughter, interruptions, protests, more laughter and then the reins of the story being picked up again.

Once a year, in the Christmas holidays, we went to the coast, to Newport, where most of Olive's family lived. Ross would stay for a couple of days and then return to hungry farm animals; besides, it was the bushfire season. Our mother's family seemed calm and civilised; they never shouted or interrupted each other, or exchanged scurrilous stories; sarcasm, guile and irony were foreign to their conversation. Her father, who loved poetry as well as science, maintained a huge library in his house at Newport, a treasure-cave dark with books. Our great-aunts Ethel and Janet had many paintings in their cottage, as well as handwoven rugs, painted curtains, a loom and a pottery kiln. Janet had travelled to Europe before the war but had come home early, chilled by Hitler's rallies; Olive's father had been briefly to the Antarctic with Shackleton in 1907, as a young scientist and deckhand, and in 1926 he'd travelled to China and Japan; souvenirs of all these trips were visible in both houses, enchanting evidence of the wider world.

Olive's father had a gentle manner, otherworldly rather than remote, which seemed related to his journey to the frozen end of the world. He was a professor of geology by the time we knew him. A glacier in the Antarctic bore his name; he had stood on the edge of volcanoes and gazed towards their fiery hearts: he knew how fire and ice had shaped the world. He seemed to inhabit a different time dimension to other people. Walking with his grandchildren around the Newport cliffs, he would pick up slatey stones and split them apart to show the stems of fossil planes, pressed flat like the specimens that often slipped out of our parents' botany books at home; he would put them into our hands, telling us how many millions of years ago the plants had lived. He had been introduced to the study of geology by his future wife, the grandmother we never knew, when they were both still schoolchildren; we sometimes (carefully supervised) looked at her sketchbooks of rock formations and dissected flowers, all drawn with enticing grace.

The atmosphere of Olive's family was gentle and somehow English; in Ross's family, on the other hand, the Irish rebel Patrick Pearse was a cousin of some kind; his family struck sparks off each other and lived hotly in the present, though they continually brought the past to life with stories. They had a natural resistance to convention and authority, were self-sufficient not only in the bush. Fortunately, our parents, though they argued about England, Ireland and religion, were both loyal to Labor principles and in complete political accord; a deep love of nature united them too.

Members of the Cotton family would come to the country on visits, generally towing caravans or bringing tents. Our house at Spring Forest, built in 1912, had two weatherboard rooms with a verandah back and front. Added onto the back verandah was an unlined room of corrugated iron nailed to round timber poles cut from the bush. Stowed above the fireplace at the end of this room, in which Peter and I slept, there was a suitcase through whose broken lid could be seen the gleam of glass plate negatives stacked together, from our mother's former life. On the back verandah was a cabin trunk in which she kept most of her more valued negatives and photographs. A couple of portraits of children we had never met, commissioned in studio days, adorned the corrugated walls of our room, put there by Olive as half-imaginary companions for us. They were city children, gazing out from warmly lit rooms; they came from another culture, in the time before we were born.

On the walls of the house at Spring Forest were two paintings by our friend Douglas Annand; the shelves held books and magazines from Olive's Sydney life (notably Sydney Ure Smith's *Australia* journal, in which we found pictures by both Olive and Douglas), school prizes including the *Oxford Book of English Verse,* much consulted by both parents, and a little book on nutrition by George Dupain. Ross's personal collection included *Sheep Management and Diseases, Australian Barkers and Biters* and *Faust.* His brother John, divorced from our aunt Jean Lorraine who lived in Panama, had died in a plane crash in 1953 in Papua New Guinea, and some of his books found their way to us: a treatise on childbirth, *Totem and Taboo,* various poetry books (in one of which was a photograph of an extremely gangrenous leg he'd saved from amputation, used as a bookmark). There were no books of photographs at all except for a couple of Australian yearbooks (nothing by Man Ray, Cartier Bresson or similar figures). It was an interesting collection of books, formed by different tastes; we read them all.

The Rolleiflex and its magical ability was an important presence in our everyday life, like the wireless and the refrigerator (the eyes, ears and stomach of our house); knowing how to take photographs was regarded as a most desirable skill. Olive never used any other camera; she did not like the little negatives or the eye-level viewfinders of the cameras that other people sometimes enthusiastically recommended to her. She did not take intrusive candid shots or try to catch people unawares. She looked downwards at her subjects through the Rolleiflex's bright glass focussing screen as if it were a private consideration between herself and the camera.

Olive was not much like other mothers; she never had her hair permed in the style of the times, never joined any rural groups or associations and did not surpass herself at primary school picnic days when tables groaned with a dazzling display of cakes and biscuits (she once laughingly referred to 'the awful labour of making a sponge cake'). My brother and I knew that she knew music, mathematics and photography, and were proud of her abilities. 'How's the photographing going?' neighbours would ask her from time to time, after she opened the studio in Cowra, and sometimes called upon her to help with difficult mathematical calculations.

Though she loved the bush and the countryside, Olive always preferred animals to be in their natural state and at a distance: rather a difficult viewpoint for a farmer's wife. Ross, however, could charm birds out of trees and calm injured animals while he doctored their wounds. Olive never learned, or wished to learn, to ride a horse or milk a cow, and the behaviour of dogs was distasteful to her; nor did she feel motherly towards the intemperately bleating 'poddy' lambs, brought in beside the fire in winter, that kept scrambling out of their cardboard boxes and getting under her feet while she was trying to prepare dinner. She had been on (rather than 'ridden') a horse on only three occasions, all of them unsalutory; and anyway Ross (who had been one of the riders in Charles Chauvel's 1940 film *Forty Thousand Horsemen)* knew what risky creatures horses could be; he didn't particularly want his family riding them. City visitors to Spring Forest would sometimes ask eagerly where the horses were; I would have to explain that the couple of horses we had were completely wild and not for recreation. Ross kept them for other reasons: they were descendants of long-dead, highly regarded horses from his boyhood.

Ross would bring back flowers and leaves from the bush to show us, and sometimes Olive would choose to photograph them. Both parents knew the Latin names of plants; their use of the plants' scientific names, rather than demeaning nicknames such as 'Eggs 'n' bacon', was a sign of respect for the bush and everything in it, although this was a time when it was generally accepted that trees 'robbed' the soil, when the conscientious farmer called the bush 'scrub' and trees 'timber', and destroyed as much of them as he could. An acute observer, Ross discovered the presence of several rare bird species at Spring Forest, and bird photographers came to visit and made 'hides' in the bush, which seemed to us like cubbyhouses where grown-ups played a game with birds. On car trips, we would hear our parents drawing each other's attention to certain striking trees and cloud formations. It seemed as if Ross, because his family had lived in the district for so long, knew stories attached to every feature of the landscape: a tree, for instance, might have a parrots' nest inside, or have been struck by lightning years before with a swagman camped beneath it; a roadside rock might have been run into by some old fellow in a sulky. In those enormous spaces of our childhood, all people were highly significant landmarks and even lichens and stones had character.

There was great respect for Olive's photographic skill throughout the family, but for many years there was nowhere for her to practise it beyond the immediate taking of pictures. In fact, by the time I left home at the age of eighteen, piped water and electricity (those darkroom prerequisites) had still not come to Spring Forest. We had to conserve and sometimes cart water, the old household well having run dry some years before. Our refrigerator was kerosene-powered; the house was lit by pressure lanterns. Until 1964, when Olive opened her studio in Cowra, all her negatives had simply been developed and contact-printed through chemists' shops, the exposed film often waiting many weeks to be processed.

I think that Olive enjoyed everything about the studio, except the recurrent task of photographing weddings with the inevitable anxiety that something might go wrong. Ross was a great help on these occasions, driving to the churches, carrying the cumbersome equipment and talking to the guests (he seemed to know everyone in the district, and beyond) while Olive, preoccupied, would prepare to capture the ceremony in all its vital, unrepeatable stages. In the early 1970s, she submitted some prints of flowers and landscapes to the Royal Agricultural Society's Easter show in Sydney, but they were returned rejected, and this was very disheartening to her. She supposed that her particular kind of photography must be out of date and of no interest to anyone outside her family. Our mother's photographs had always been part of our lives. The Rolleiflex negatives produced contact prints quite large enough to pore over: they amplified our childhood memories like the marvellous stories told by Ross, his mother, father, brothers and sister, while the large and luminous photographs of flowers and teacups, published in old magazines, were windows on a different world.

In the early 1980s, to her surprise and delight, Olive was 'rediscovered' (though we had never realised she was lost) as scholarly attention turned to the work of forgotten women photographers. She was freed from the weddings by a grant from the Australia Council and began printing her own work again. It is fortunate that the art she discovered in childhood was photography, for this can be done in two stages: first the taking of the pictures and then, perhaps years later, the slow, thoughtful process of printing in a proper darkroom. In the way we lived then, no man or woman would have had time or space for painting, say, or writing; there was no such luxurious thing as a room of one's own.

In retrospect, our way of life in the bush seems unclassifiable, with its practical difficulties and some war-smoke high overhead in the clear blue skies, all acted upon by complicated family temperaments. Olive's photographs, before and after her life in the city, are similarly hard to pin down. They seem formed less by artistic movements and trends than by her deep attachment to nature and the inheritance she got from both her parents: an observer's eye, poetic and scientific at the same time. And perhaps by a tranquil sense of what geologists call 'deep' time, so that nature seems enduring, unlimited and at least as remarkable as transitory human life.

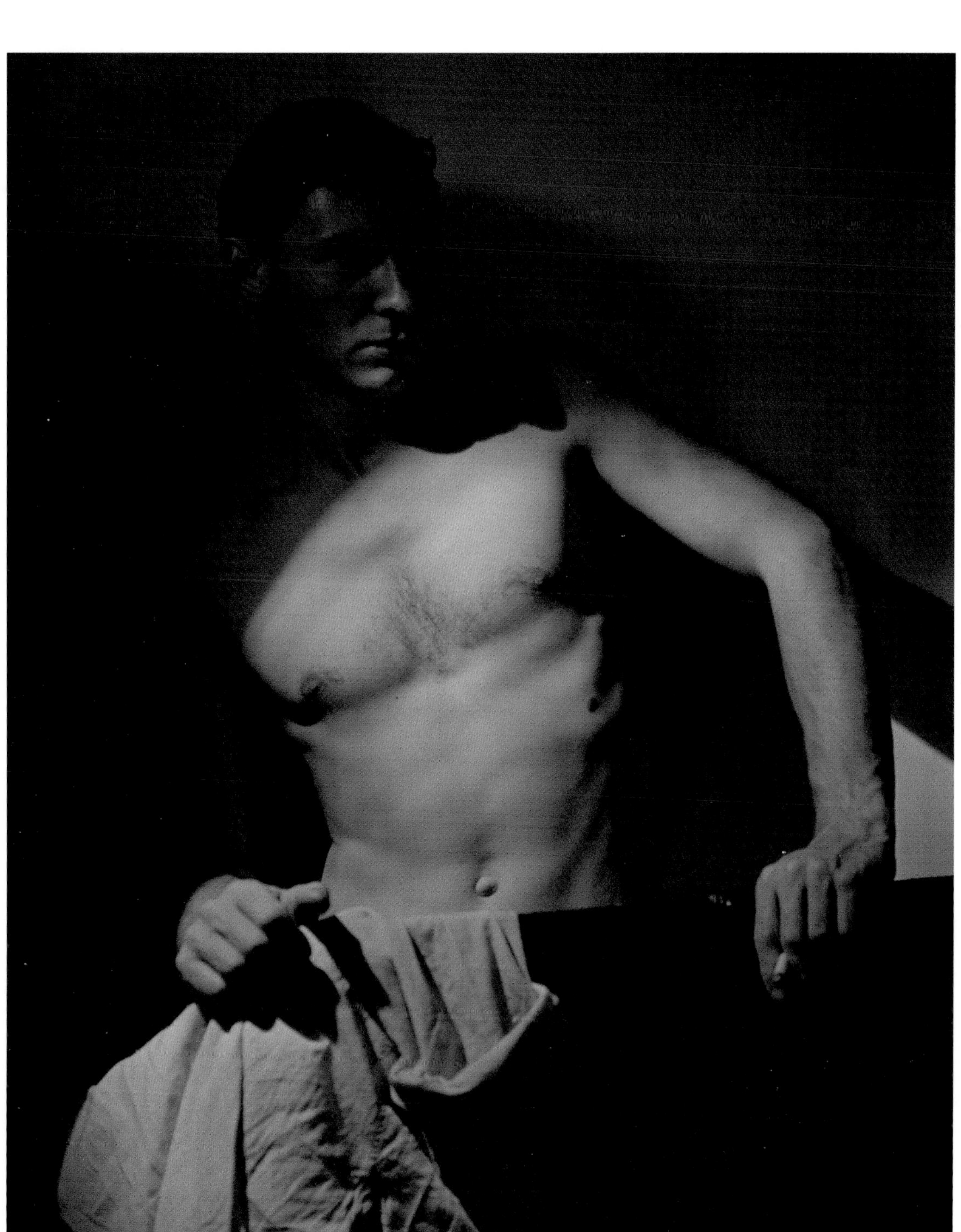

Max after surfing 1939
[National Gallery of Australia]

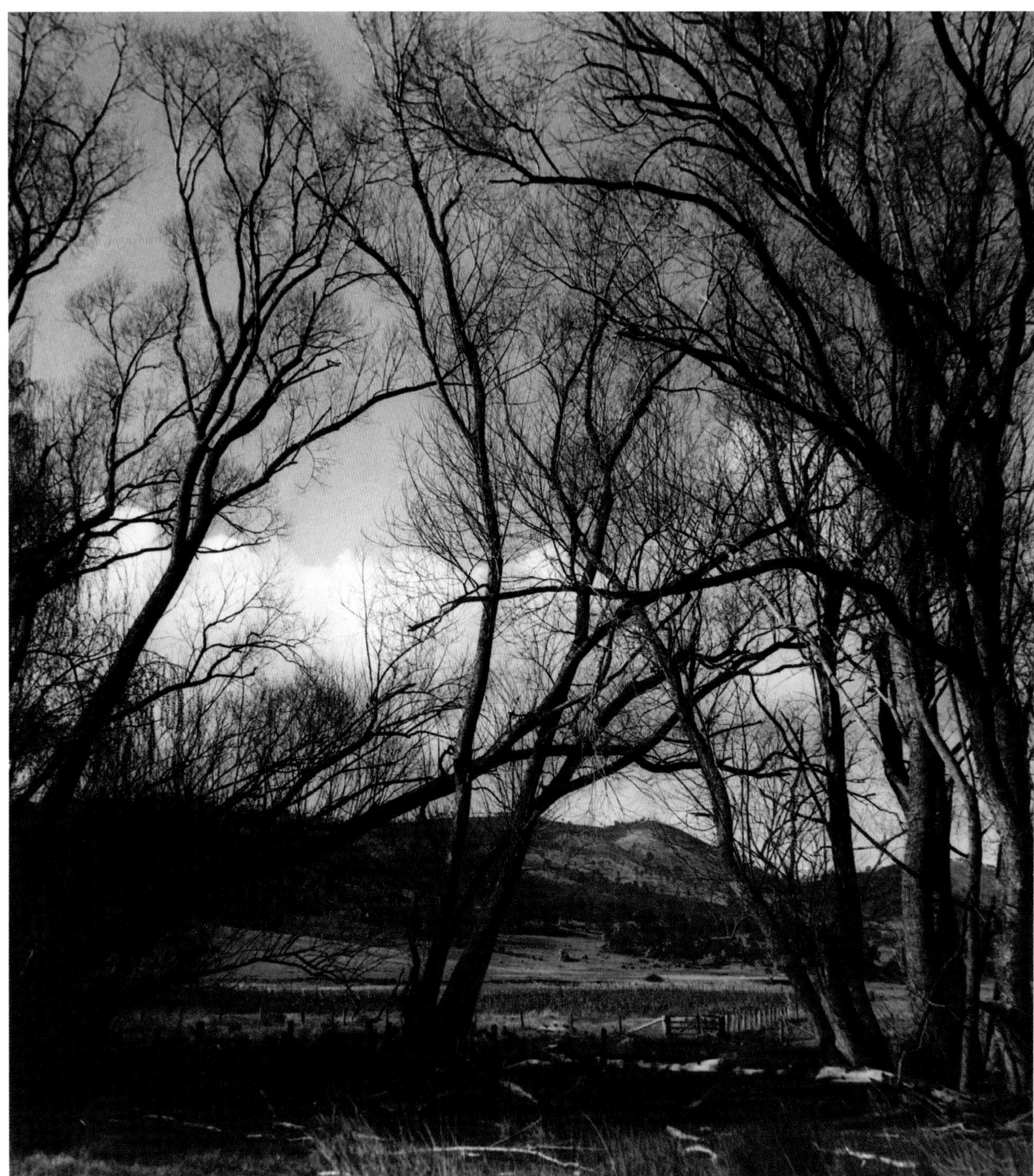

Winter willows 1937

In the autumn of 1937, I went with my father, my uncle Frank Cotton and his son Keith on a ten-day camping trip, going from Sydney up the north coast to Coffs Harbour, then across to the New England tableland and back to Sydney by the inland route. We travelled in a 1918 Buick and (generally) slept in sleeping bags under the stars. I had just bought my first Rolleiflex, and my patient father kindly stopped whenever I wanted to take a photograph. This sometimes took quite a long time—waiting for the sun and clouds to be right, selecting a viewpoint and so on.

This picture of willows was taken at Bendemeer near one of our camping places on the New England tableland. The strong lines of their trunks and main limbs gave a sense of stability amongst the general tangle of finer branches. The sky helped too.

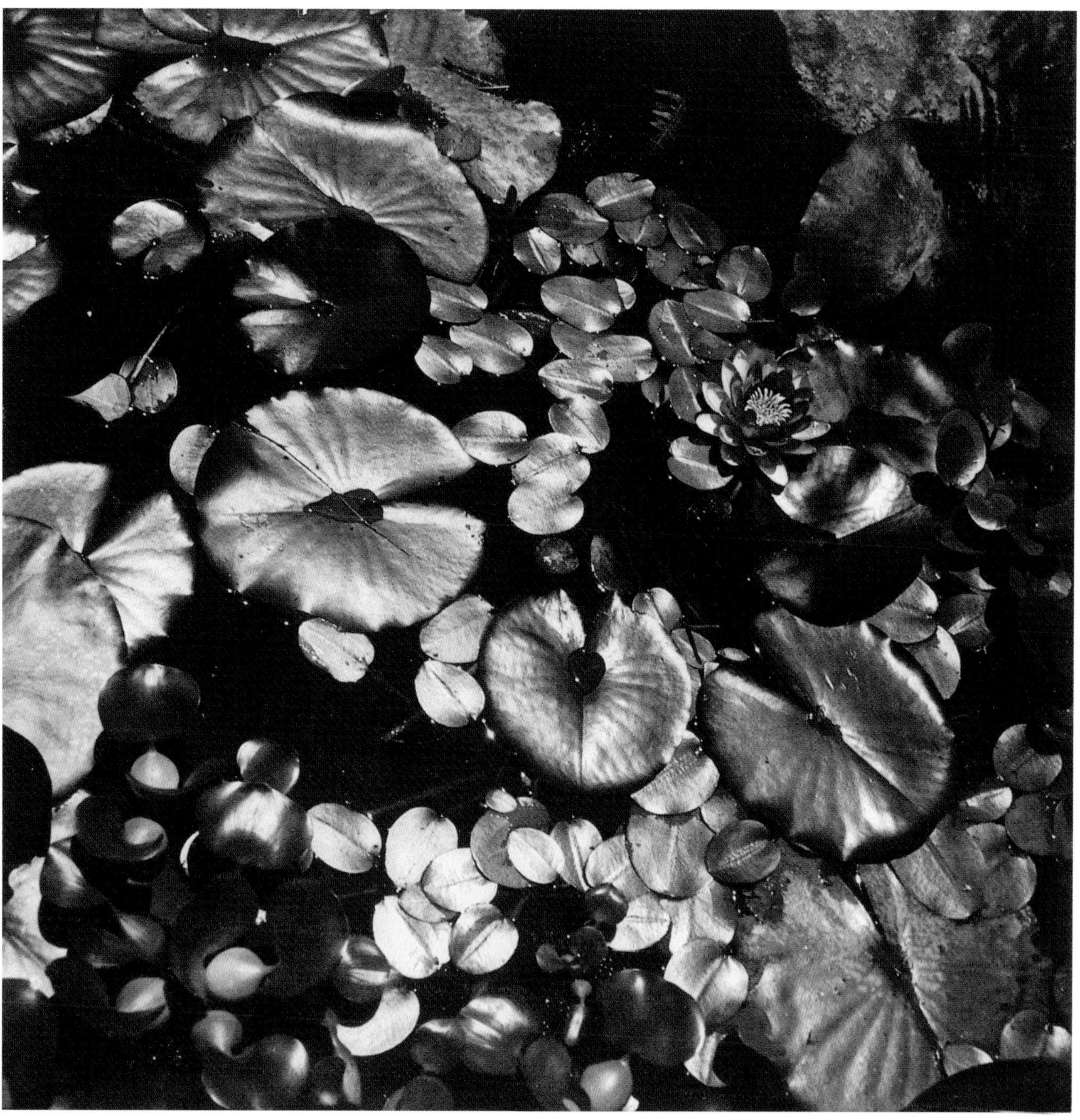

Lily pond 1938
I was attracted by the unusual light falling on the surface of the pond in my uncle Max's garden (now, incidentally, known as Lisgar Gardens and administered by Hornsby Shire Council). The light made the waterlily leaves appear almost metallic, in contrast to the fragility of the lone flower rising from them.

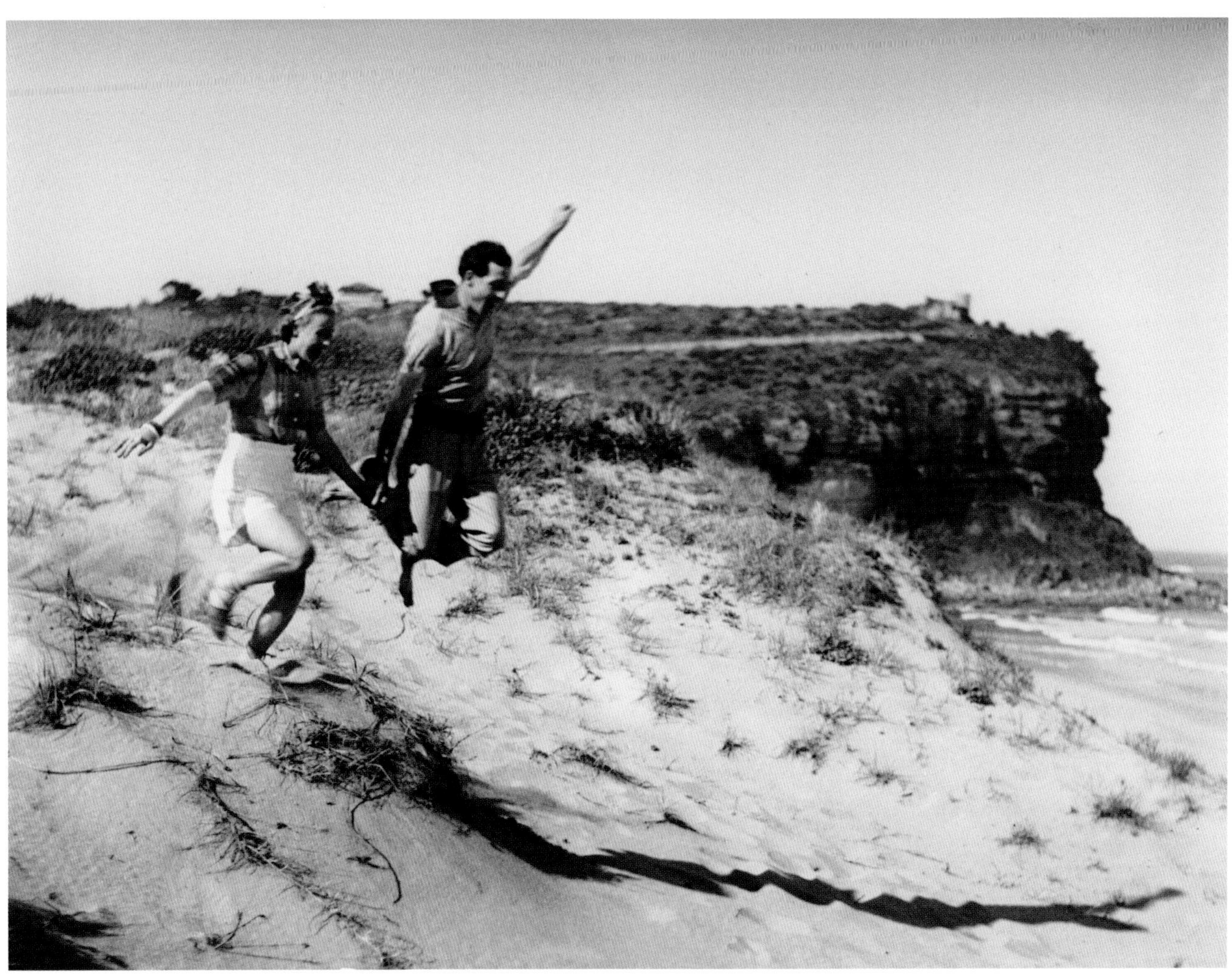

Beach snapshot 1938

This snapshot of Damien Parer and Phyl Riley was taken at Bungan Beach after a fashion shoot for a David Jones' catalogue. There was often a little light-hearted action between shots.

In these carefree days, none of us imagined that in a few years time Damien would be an accredited war photographer involved in the New Guinea campaign.

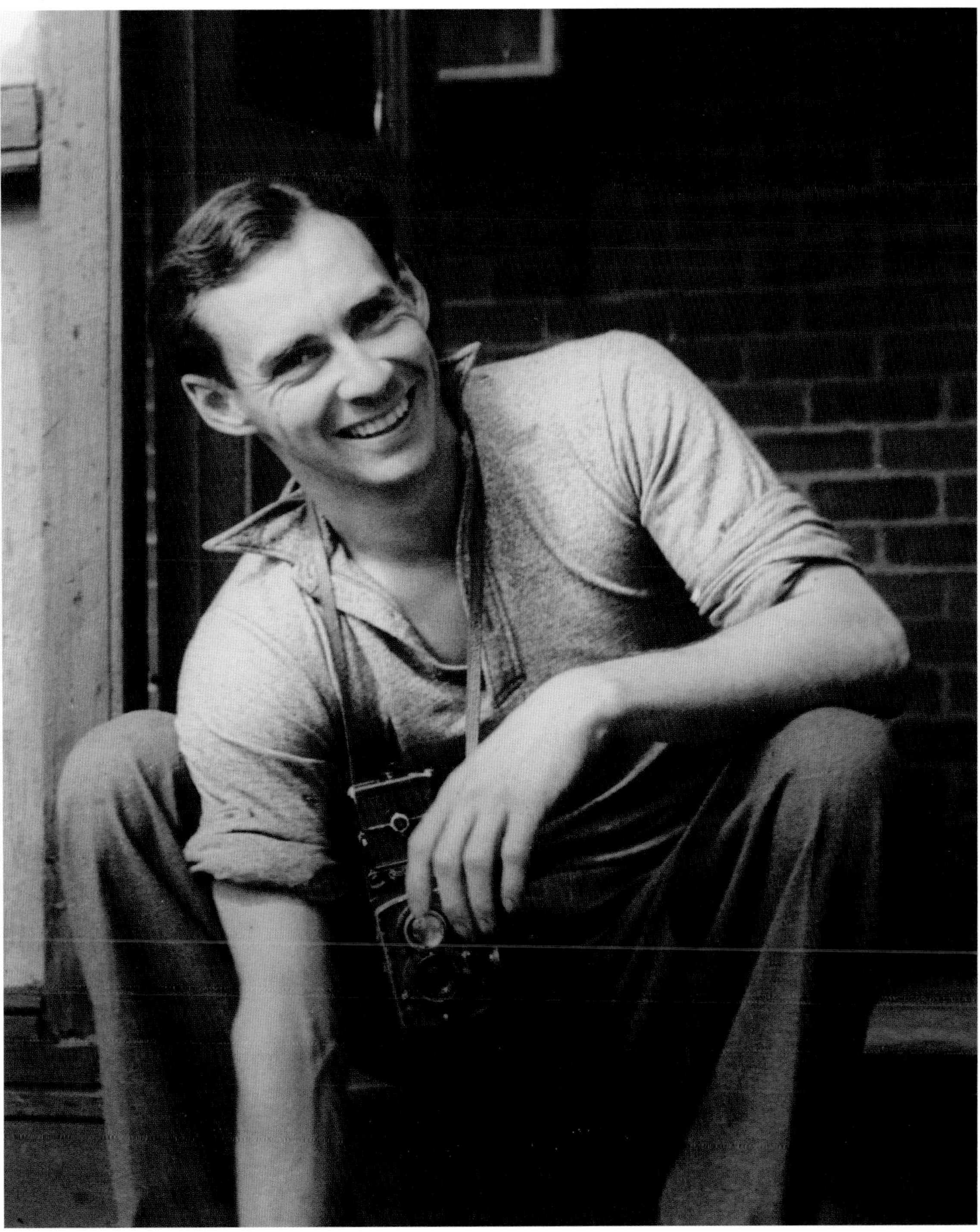

Max Dupain 1938
I like this happy picture of Max on the back steps of our house at Longueville with, as always, his camera at hand.

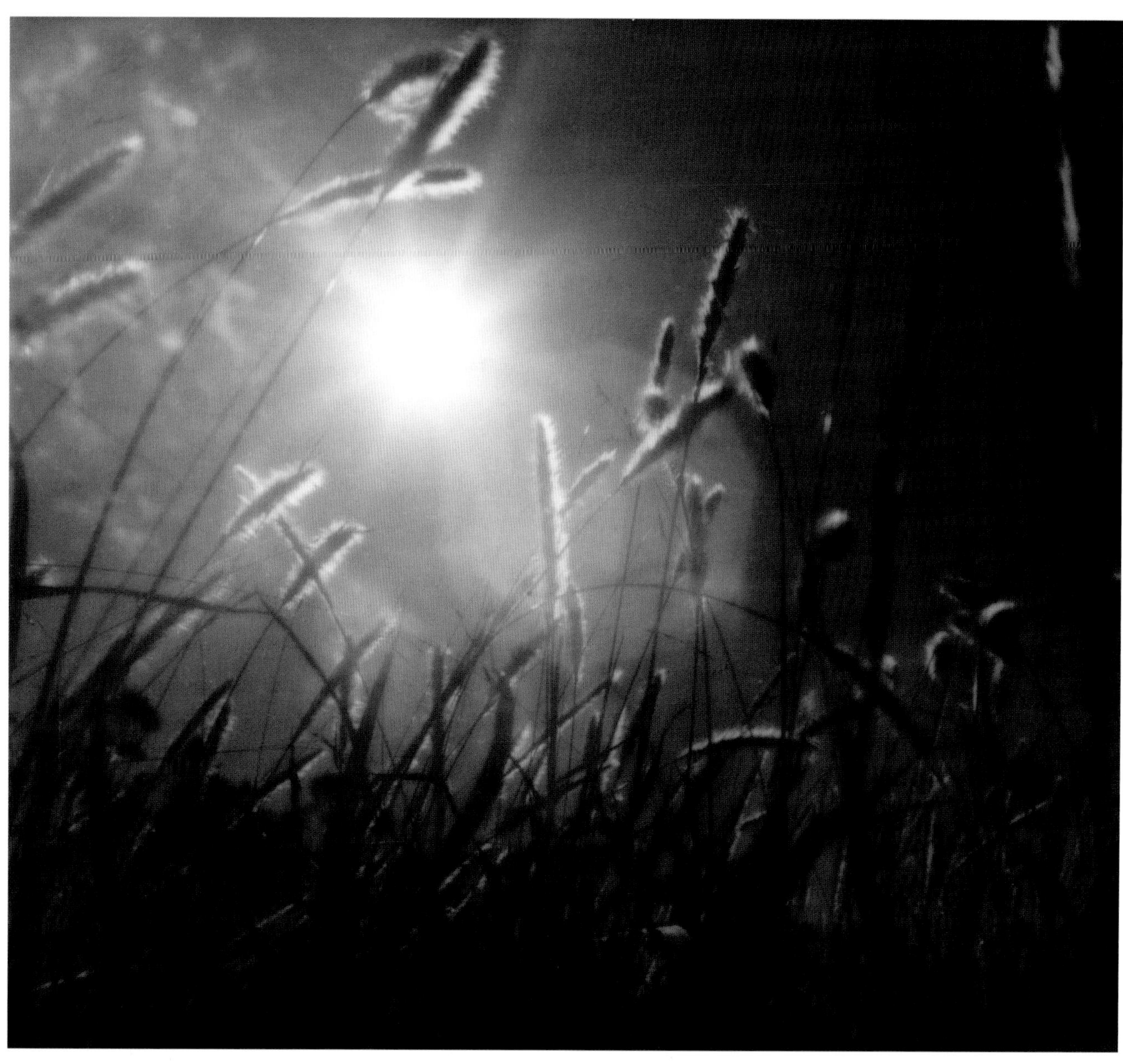

Grass at sundown 1939
[National Gallery of Australia, gift of the artist 1987]
Each grass head outlined by a nimbus of light from the setting sun and the sun's rays themselves all create, for me, a magical atmosphere.

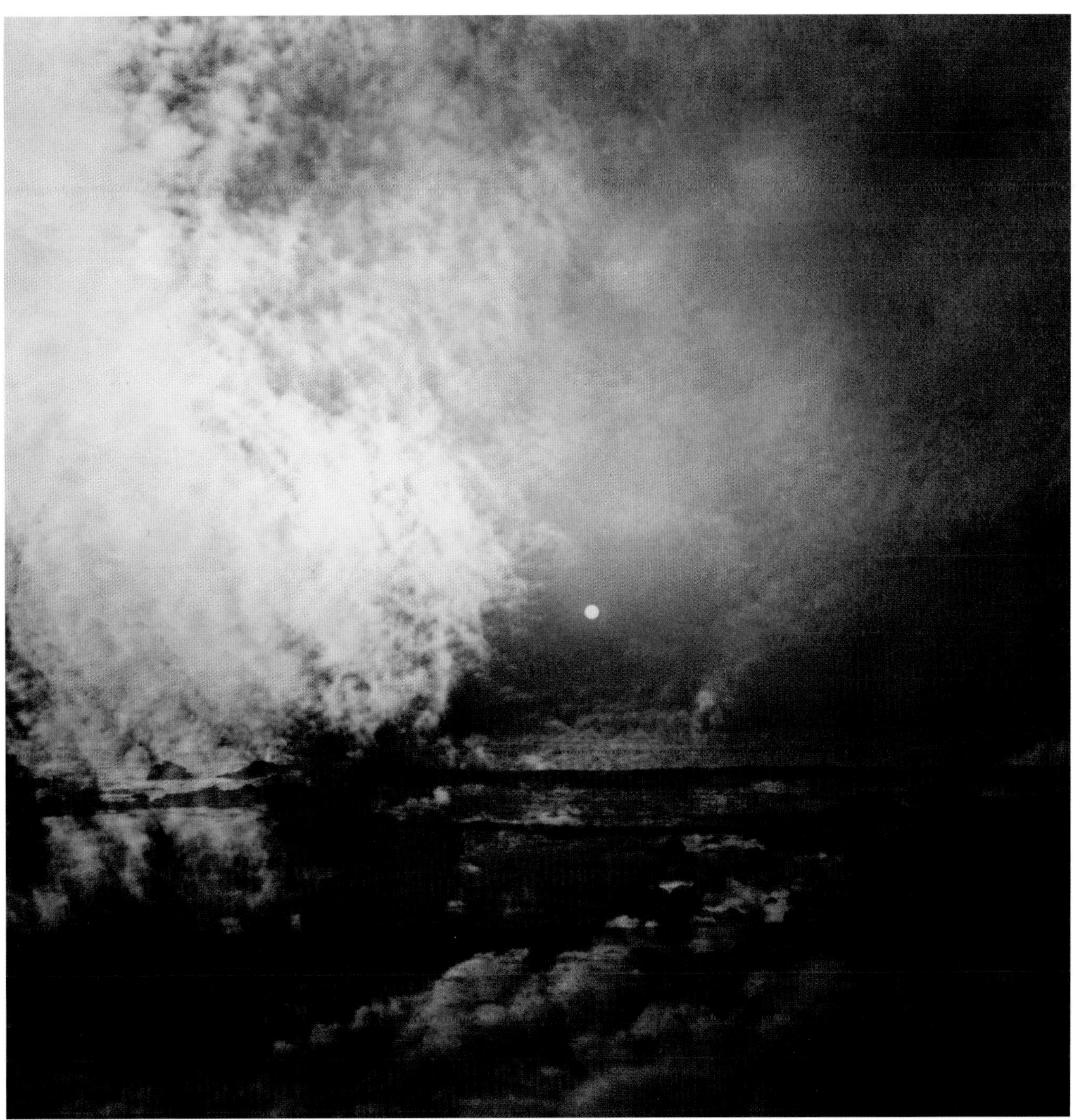

Sky submerged 1937
I had two negatives, one of an interesting sky and one of the sea. Each seemed incomplete, so I combined them until I had a satisfying composition, and the title suggested itself.

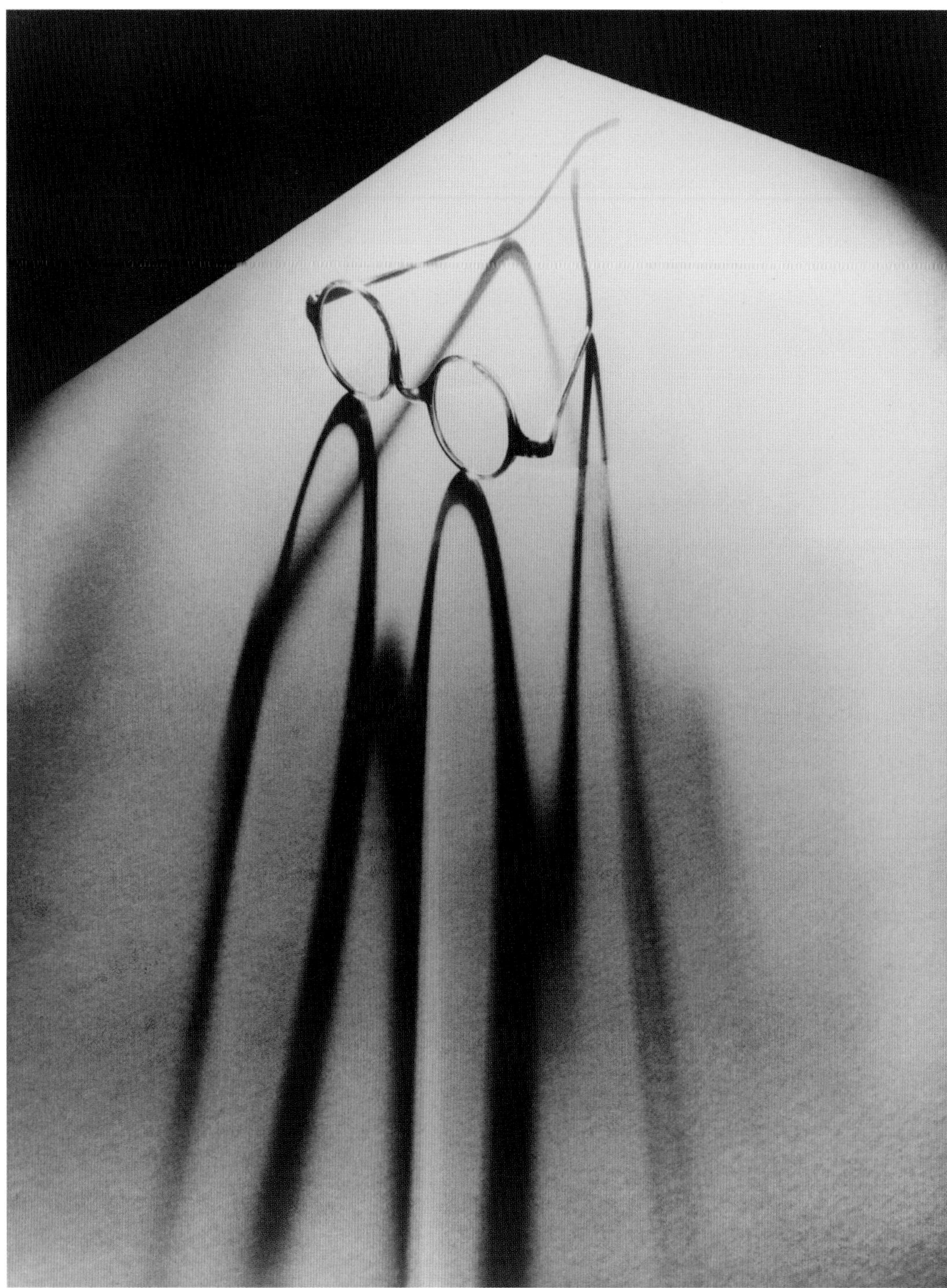

Glasses 1937
This photograph was commissioned as an advertisement for spectacle frames.
I tried to make it more interesting by using a spotlight to cast long shadows.

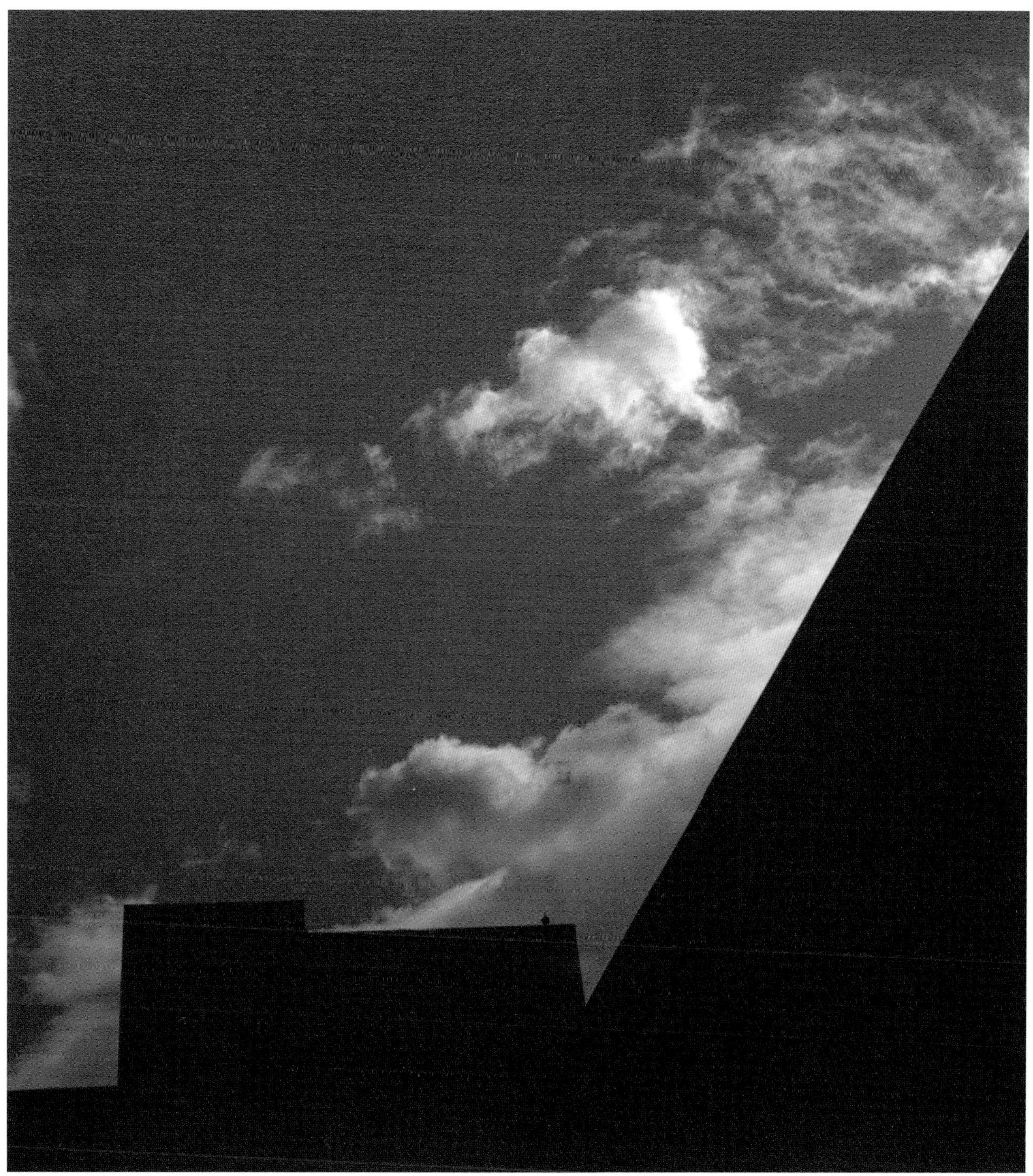

Escape 1937

It was a windy day, and I had wandered with my camera through an unfamiliar part of the city almost enclosed by the backs of buildings. The dramatic shapes of the buildings had attracted me, but they began to seem forbidding and oppressive. Nobody else was in sight, and I had a sudden fear that I would not be able to find my way out again. When some white clouds appeared, moving swiftly behind the silhouetted buildings, my panic vanished and I concentrated on photographing the clouds in their flight. Then, feeling pleased with my shot, I 'escaped' like the clouds and found my way out of the shadowy maze.

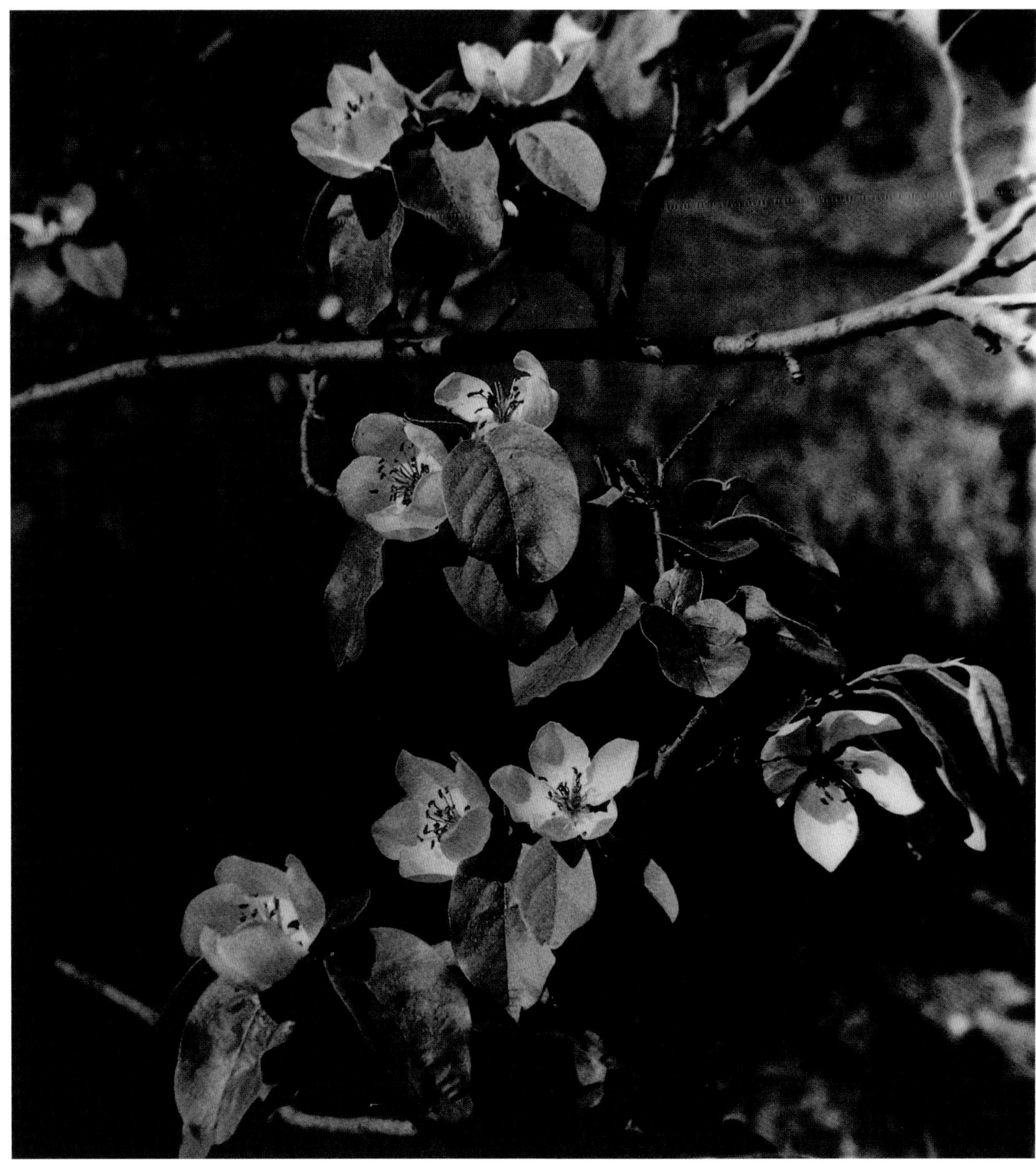

Quince blossom 1992
I photographed these blossoms on the tree, just as they were. Having selected my viewpoint, I waited until the sun was in the right position to bring out the subtle cones of light and shade, thus avoiding the appearance of stark white flowers.

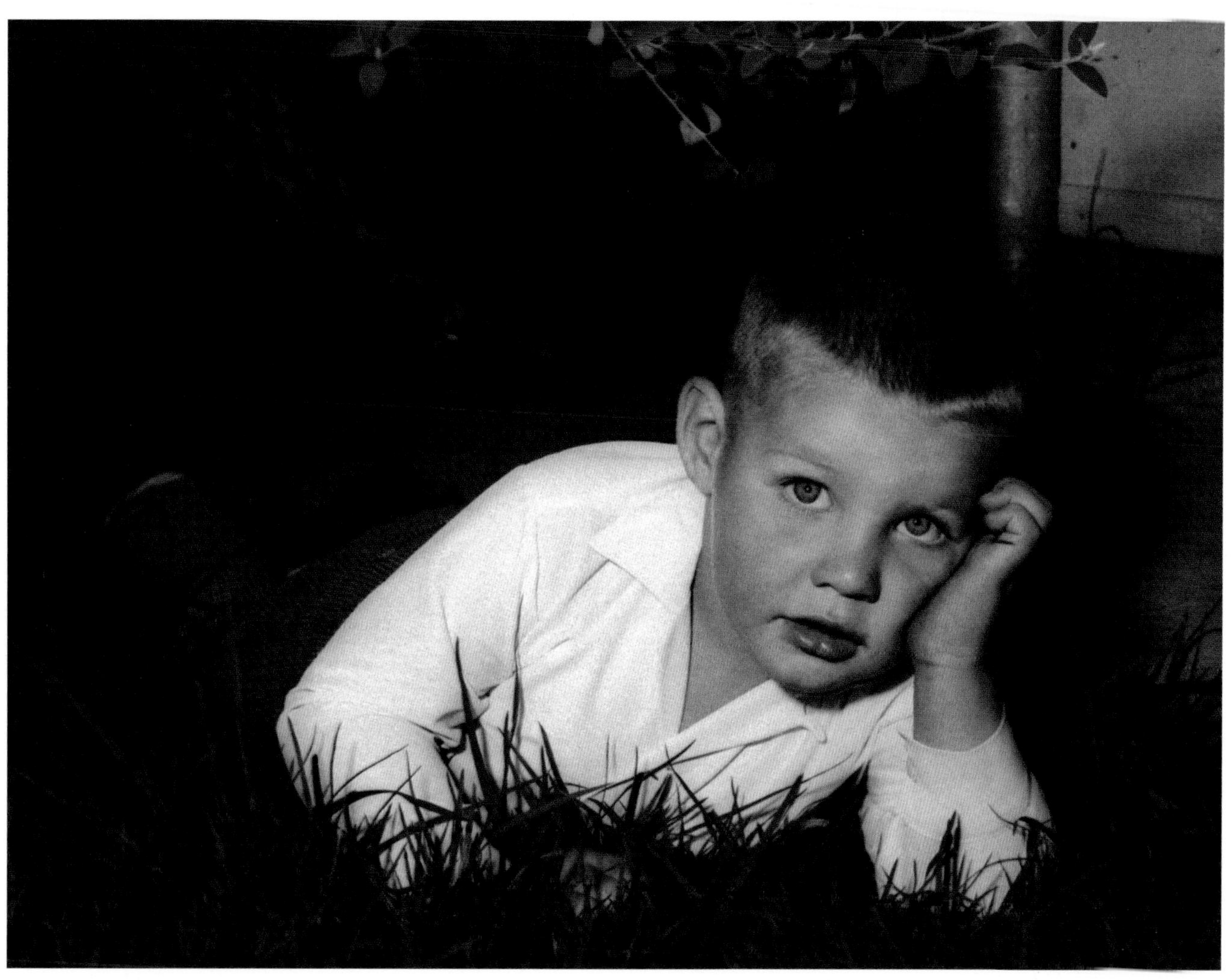

I'm a whale c.1965

Studio work in the country town of Cowra meant that I was often commissioned to photograph debutantes, weddings and children. I have always preferred to photograph other people's children out of doors at their own homes, where the surroundings are familiar to them. Commissioned to take his portrait, I followed this active little boy around his garden for what seemed like hours, until finally he threw himself down on the grass, looking up at me for a couple of seconds and announcing, 'I'm a whale'.

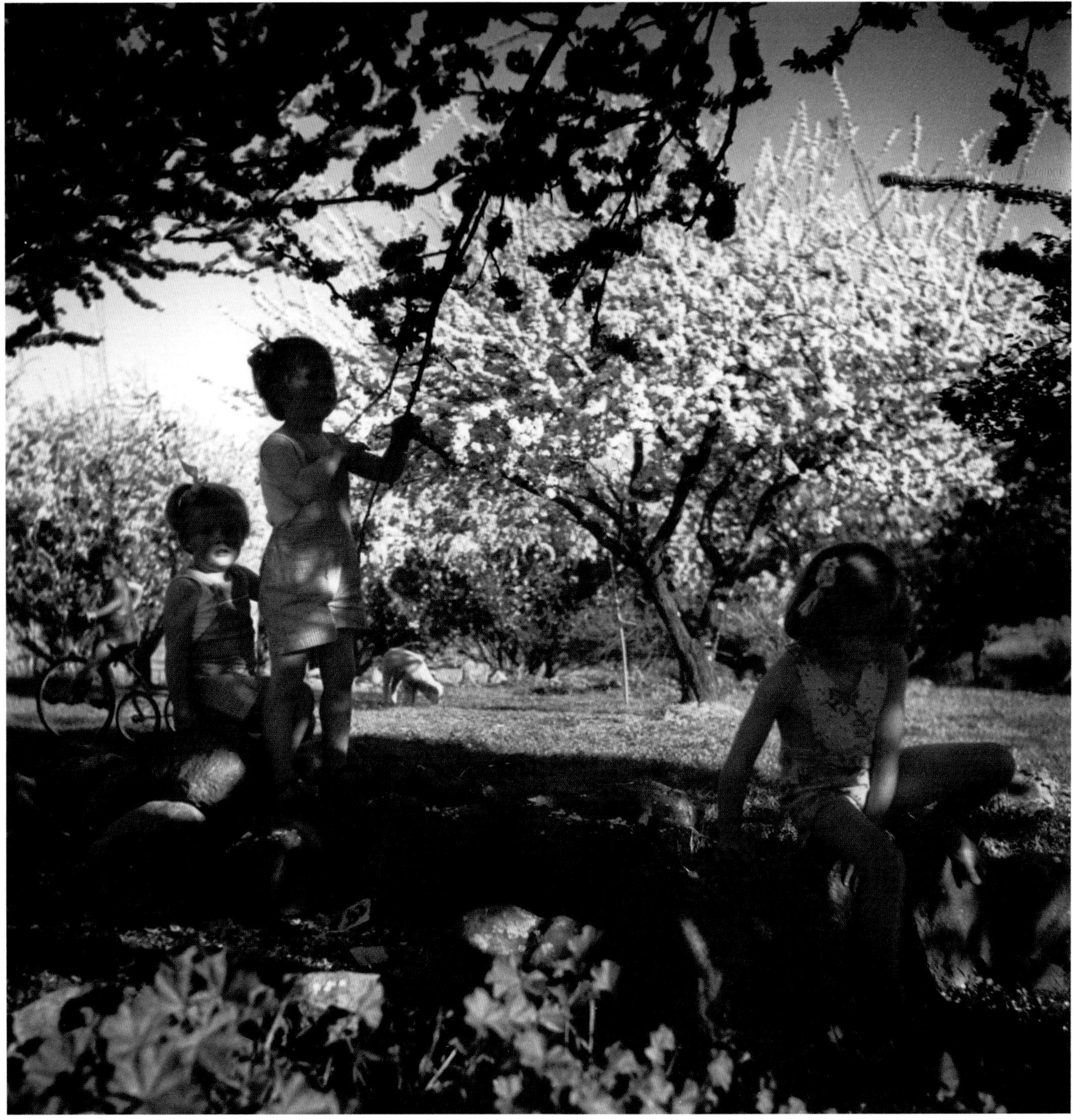

Children's garden 1952

[National Gallery of Australia]

A magnificent flowering plum tree in a neighbour's orchard attracted me to the spot where my children and their friends were all absorbed in their own pursuits on this beautiful spring day. It seemed a paradise garden where children could do as they pleased.

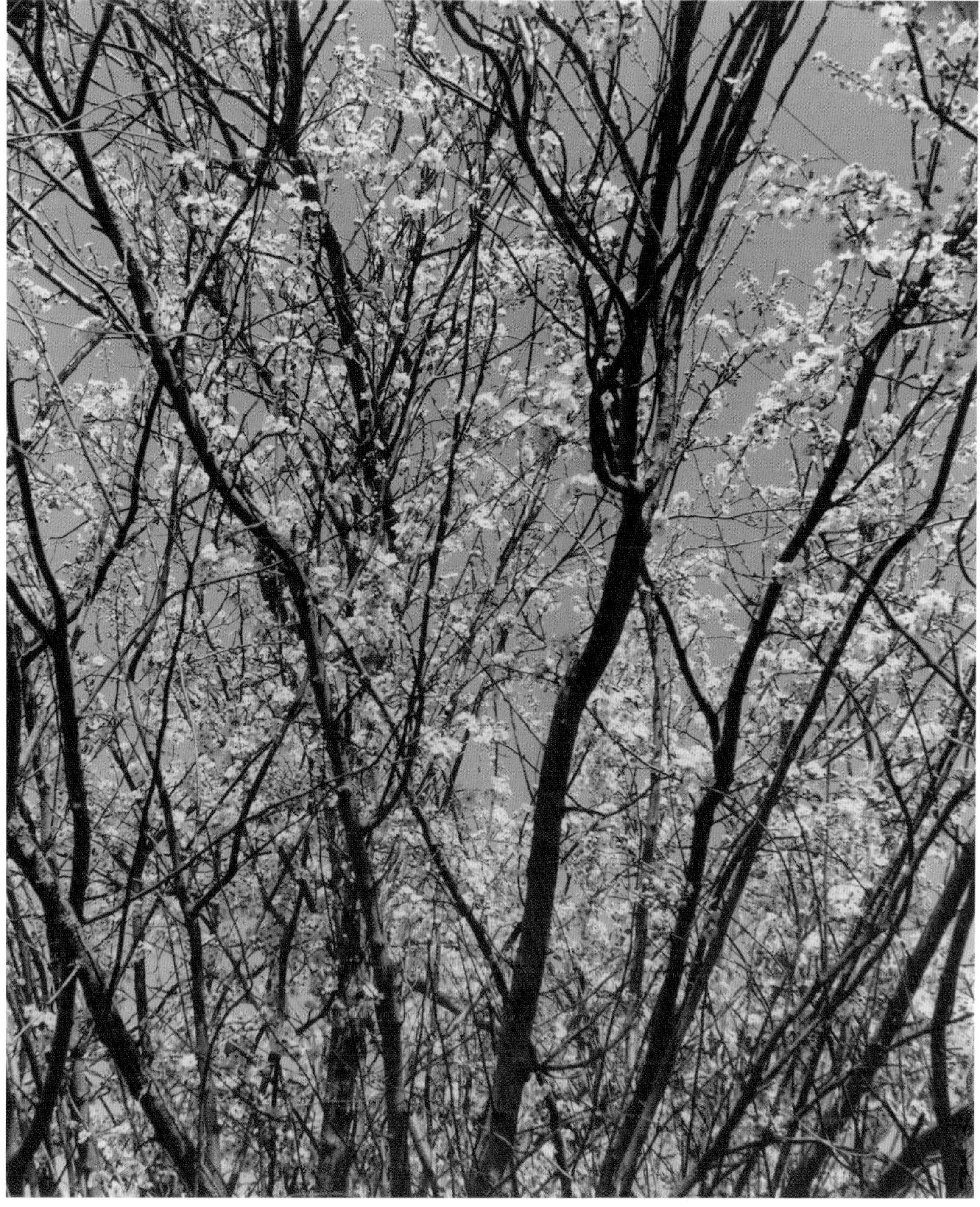

Wild plum 1984
This was a small neglected plum tree which had never been pruned, so instead of growing in formal dense heads, its flowers were scattered freely throughout the branches, catching the sunlight with a sense of happy abandon.

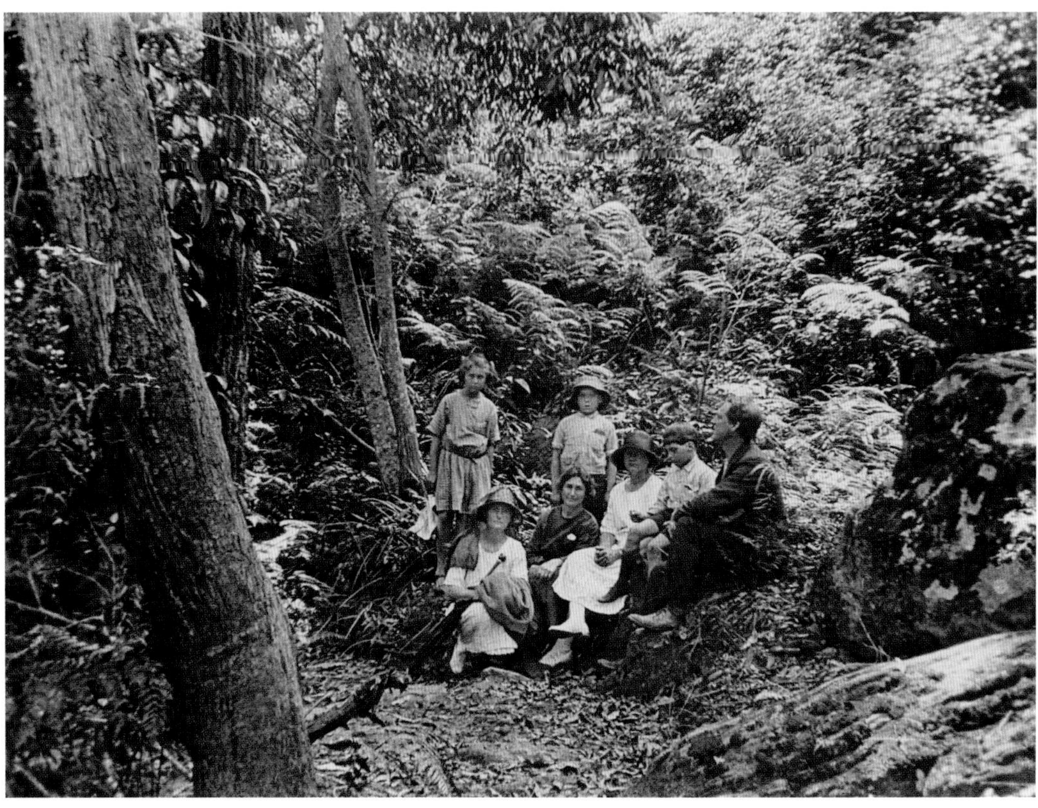

On bush track, Newport 1924

This photograph was taken with my first camera, a Kodak No.0 Box Brownie. When I was eleven, my youngest aunt, Janet Cotton, having been given a new camera, asked me if I'd like her old Box Brownie. Up until then I had been rather frustrated by what I felt was my lack of ability to paint and draw (my sister Joyce being the 'artistic' one, while I was the 'musical' one). Photography had not occurred to me as a means of expression, but when I started using the camera I felt that it was my medium. I carried the camera about in the garden, in the bush, on holidays—suddenly I felt free and able to compose pictures. It was a great awakening, being able to express myself.

This bush track (now a tarred and busy road) is in the Newport area and connects the ocean beach side to the calm Pittwater side of the district. This group consists of my sister Joyce, brother Jim, younger brother Frank, my father at far right and my mother, hatless, with her oldest sister Alice.

On my mother's right is Miss Lilian Reed who had courageously left her home to come by ship with a group of other young English women on an assisted passage, on the understanding that each would be employed as a domestic help in the Sydney suburbs of this unknown land. My father went to see if somebody suitable might be found amongst the group of newly arrived young women to help with the large household. According to family lore, he saw Miss Reed and chose to speak to her first, and she later told me that when she met my father she thought, This is a good man.

So she was engaged as our Lady Help, and came to live with us. Until we children were grown up, we always called her 'Miss Reed'; later she became 'Lilian'. But by 1929 she was homesick and decided to return to her family in England.

In 1930, my mother died of cancer, aged only forty-six. Eventually, in desperation, my father wrote to Lilian asking if she would come back to us; she returned and stayed on through all our school and university days. One by one we left home until finally, in 1949, my youngest brother was about to leave and Lilian said to my father: 'When he goes I shall have to leave too, it wouldn't be proper for me to stay on'.

My father, who had always treated her with great courtesy, was devastated—she had become part of the family, and he had never anticipated such a move. Then the solution dawned on him: he asked her to marry him, and so she became our stepmother.

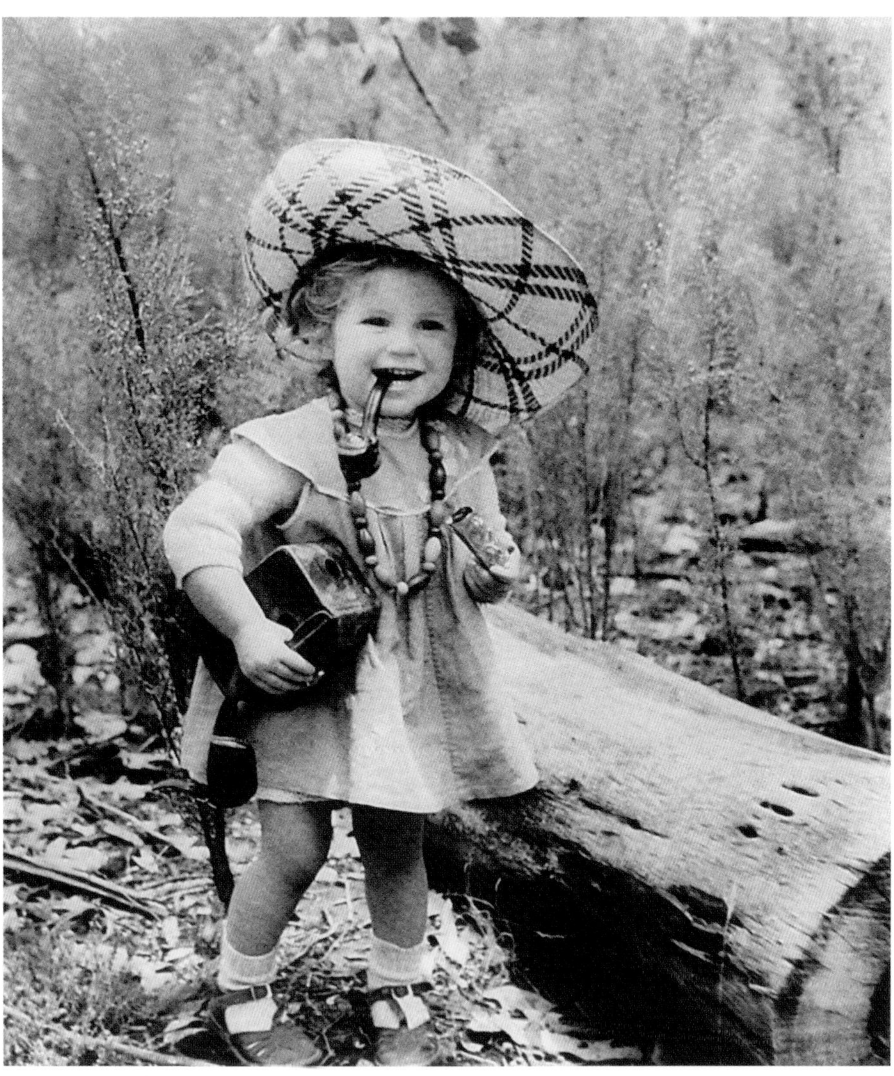

Sally 1949
Here Sally, among trees near our canvas home, has 'borrowed' my hat, my camera case and Ross's pipe, which he had rashly put down on a log—her eyes sparkling with mischief.

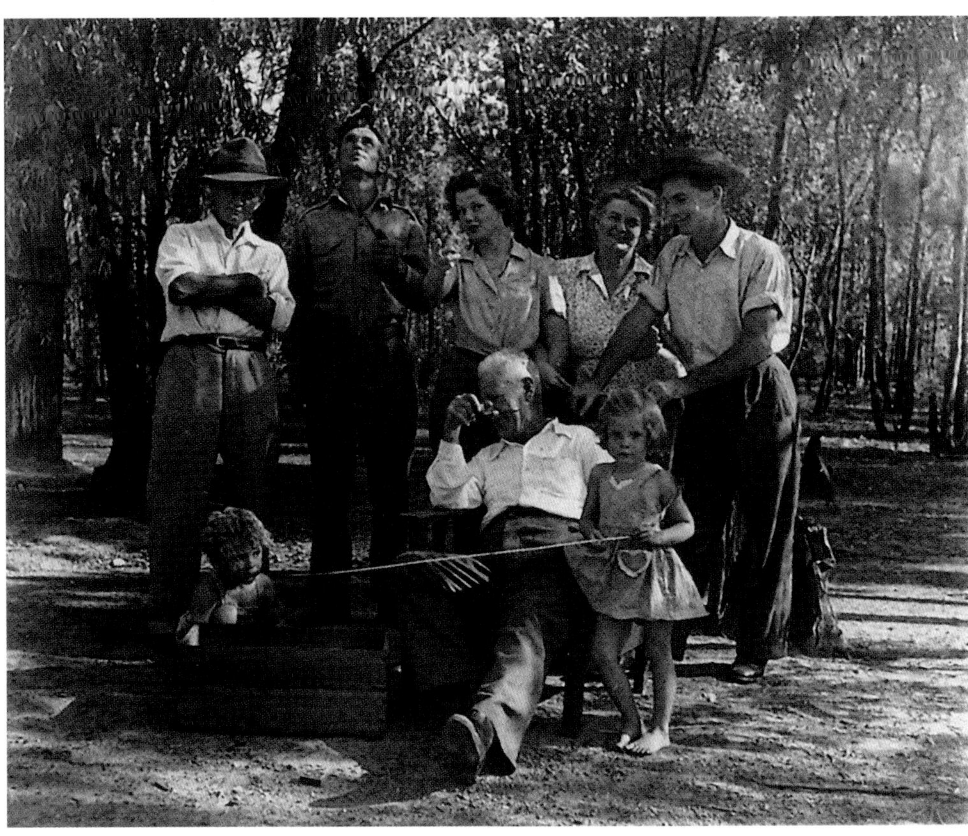

Family group on the Illunie Range 1950
Ross (second from left) with some of his family.
Just visible on the left is part of the stringybark hut.

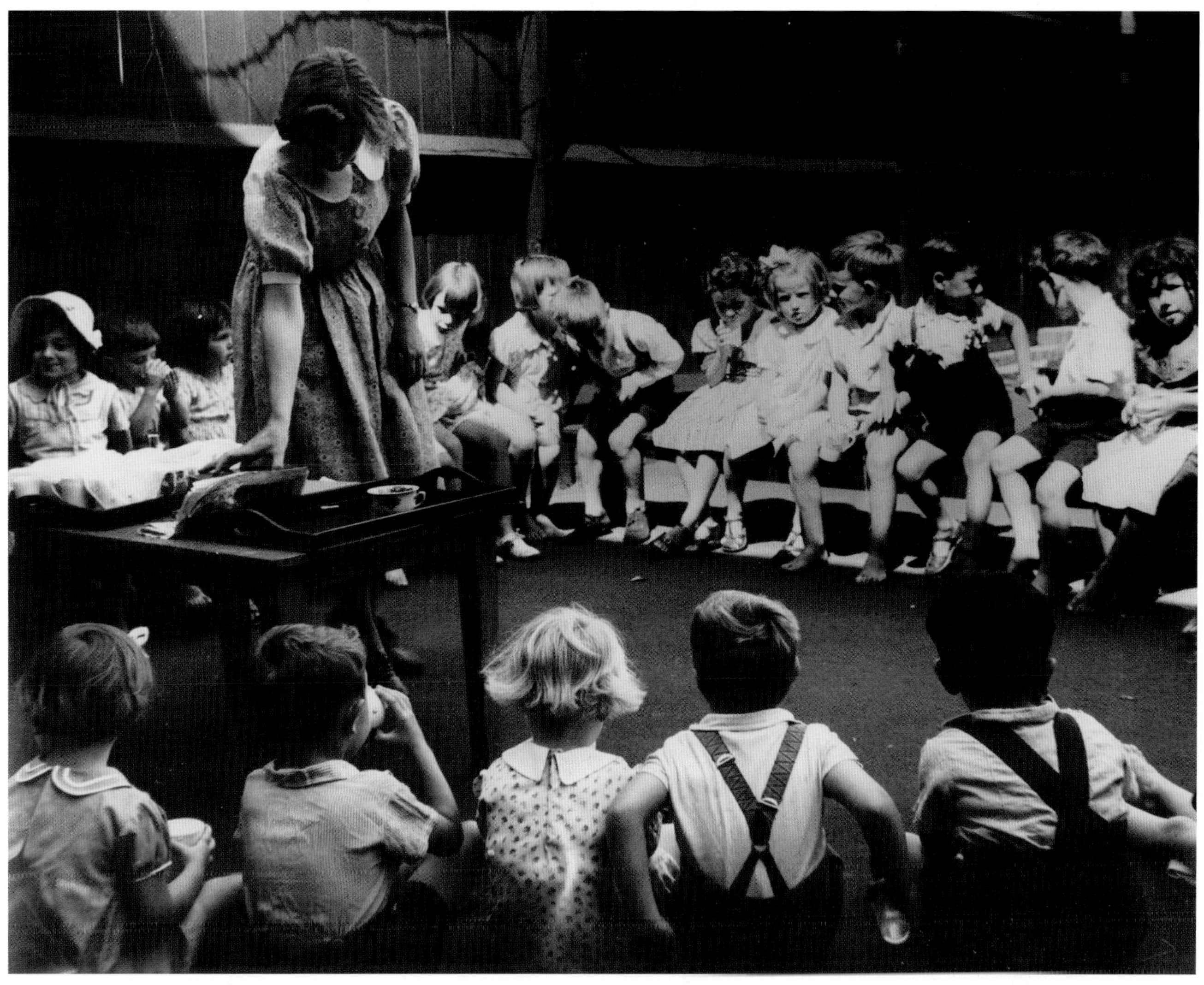

Woolloomooloo Free Kindergarten c.1939

[National Gallery of Australia]

I was asked by my aunt Ethel Cotton, who was a primary school teacher and keen educationist, if I could take a series of photographs as an informal record of this kindergarten. Its equipment was minimal. The playground was paved with asphalt; there was a high cement wall along one side and a paling fence along another part of the boundary. In this photograph the children are sitting on wooden benches waiting to be given their drinks of milk at morning recess. Some are barefoot; there was no attempt to impose a school uniform here, as many families would have been unable to afford it. There seemed to be a happy understanding between the children and the fully trained staff.

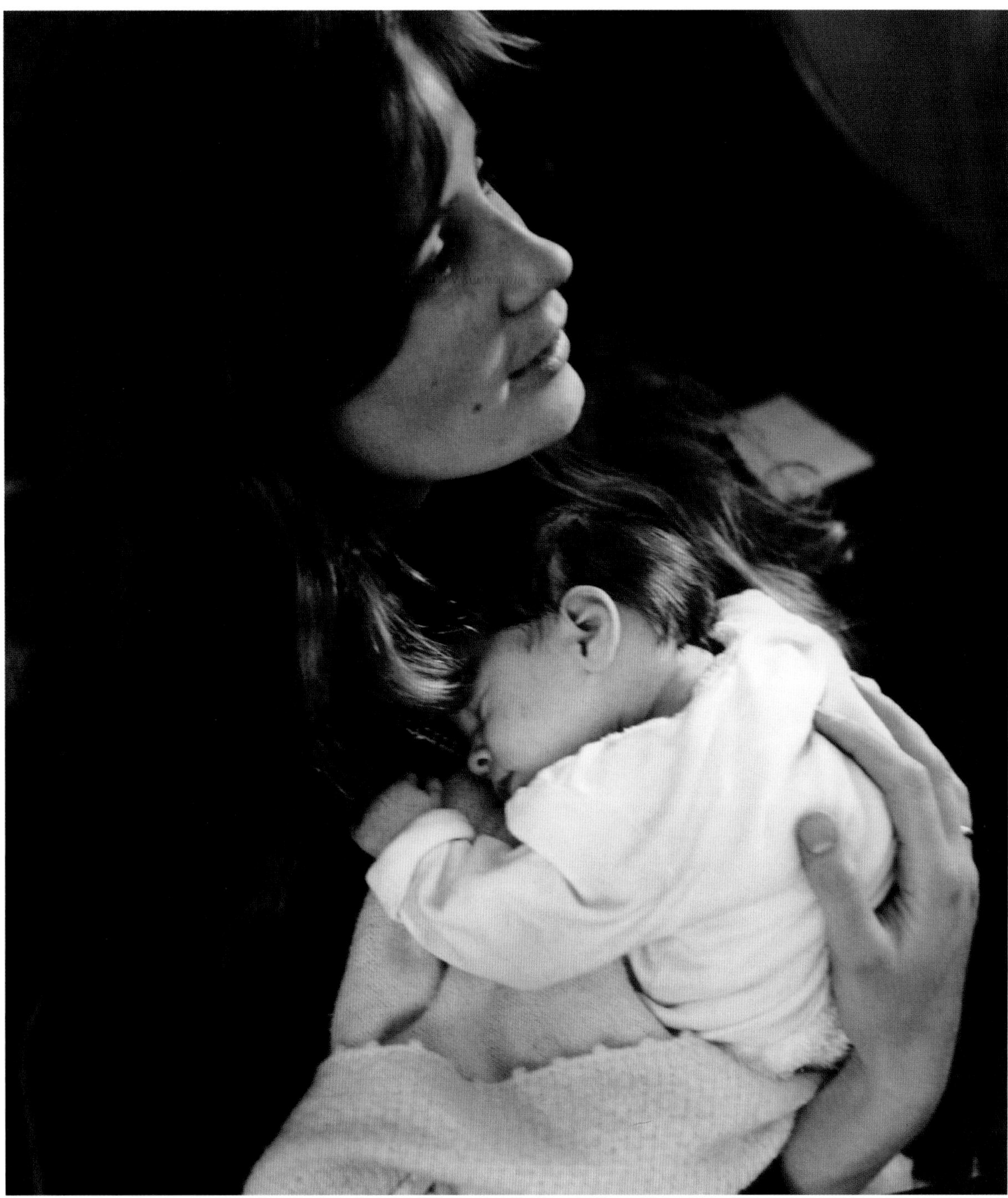

My daughter and grand–daughter 1971
This is a photograph of Sally with our first grandchild, Julia, when she was six weeks old. It was taken in soft light, by a window—a sleeping baby nestling against her mother.

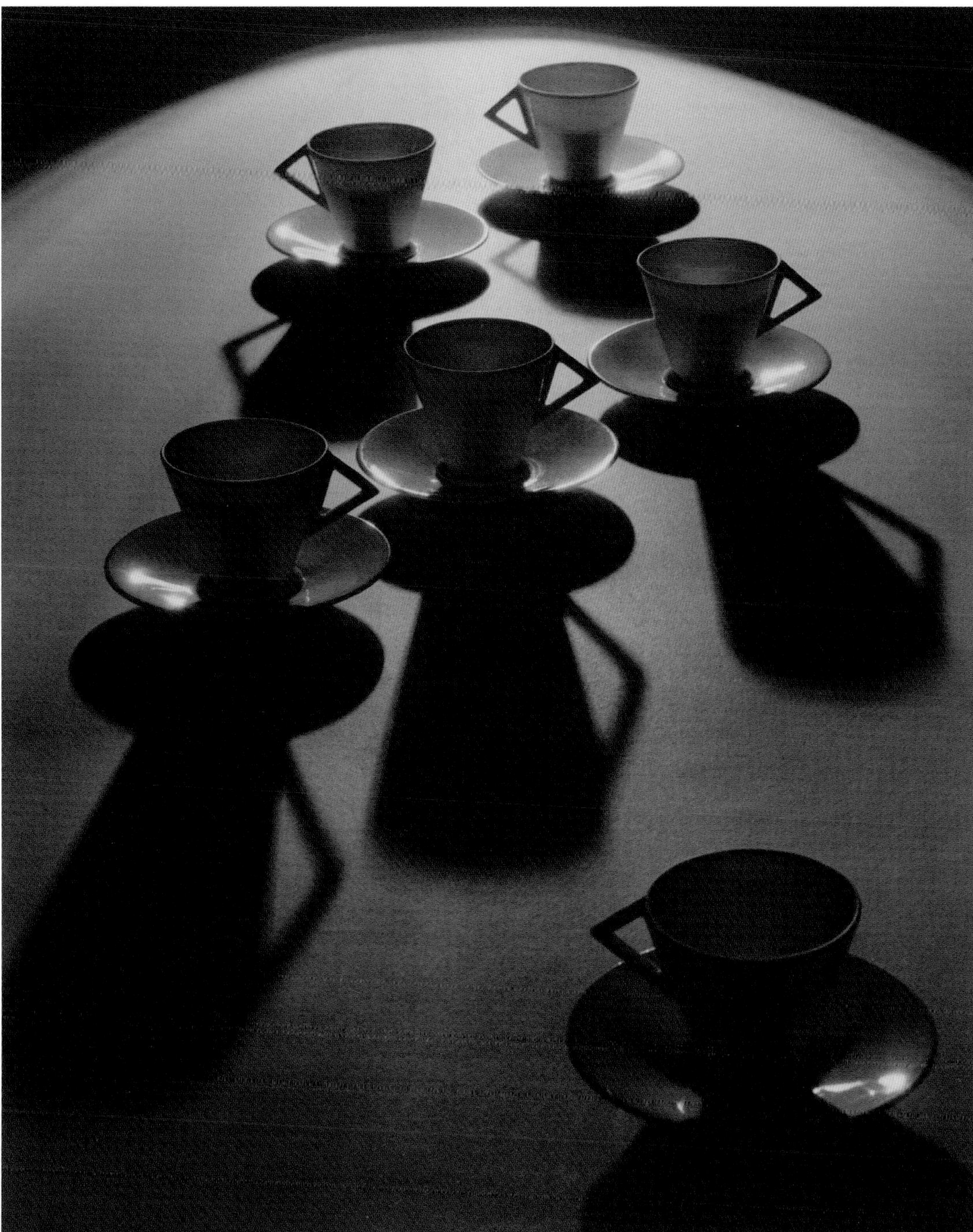

Teacup ballet 1935

[National Gallery of Australia]

This picture evolved after I had bought some inexpensive cups and saucers from Woolworths for our studio coffee breaks to replace our rather worn old mugs, no longer suitable for offering to visitors. The angular handles reminded me of arms akimbo, and that led to the idea of making a photograph to express a dance theme.

When the day's work was over I tried several arrangements of the cups and saucers to convey this idea, without success, until I used a spotlight and realised how important the shadows were. Using the studio camera, which had a 6 ½ x 4 ½, inch ground glass focussing screen, I moved the cups about until they and their shadows made a ballet-like composition and then photographed them on a cut film negative. Then the title of the photograph suggested itself. This was my first photograph to be shown overseas, being exhibited, to my delight, in the London Salon of Photography in 1935.

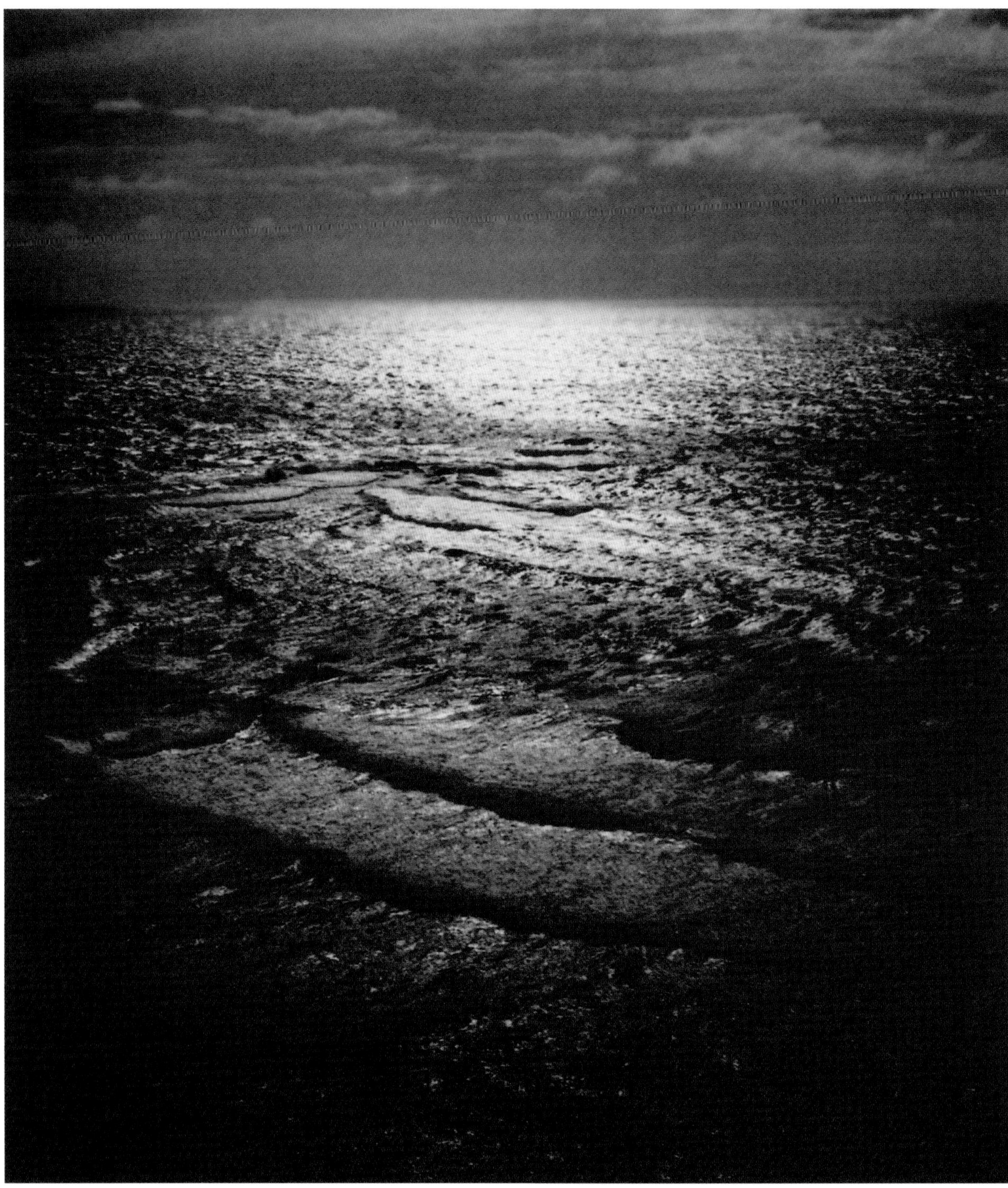

The sea's awakening 1937
This photograph was taken from the southern headland of Newport Beach. It was early morning, before the sun rose, and soft daylight accented every ripple of the water.

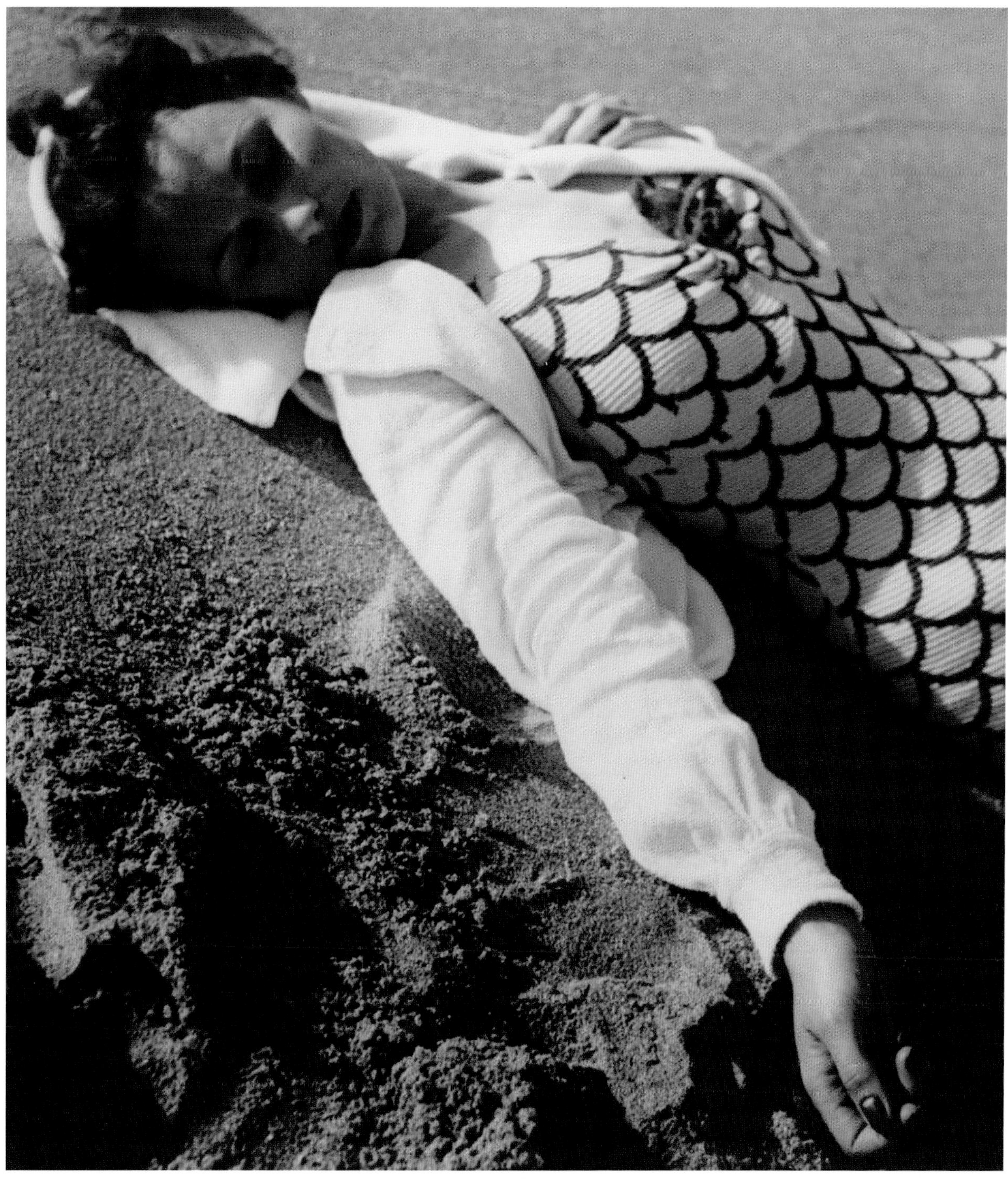

Beachwear fashion shot c.1938

The model here is Phyl Riley. This shot was taken on Bungan Beach when Damien Parer and Max Dupain were photographing models in the new season's beachwear for David Jones's summer catalogue. I amused myself with my camera while Max and Damien attended to the serious demands of fashion photography.

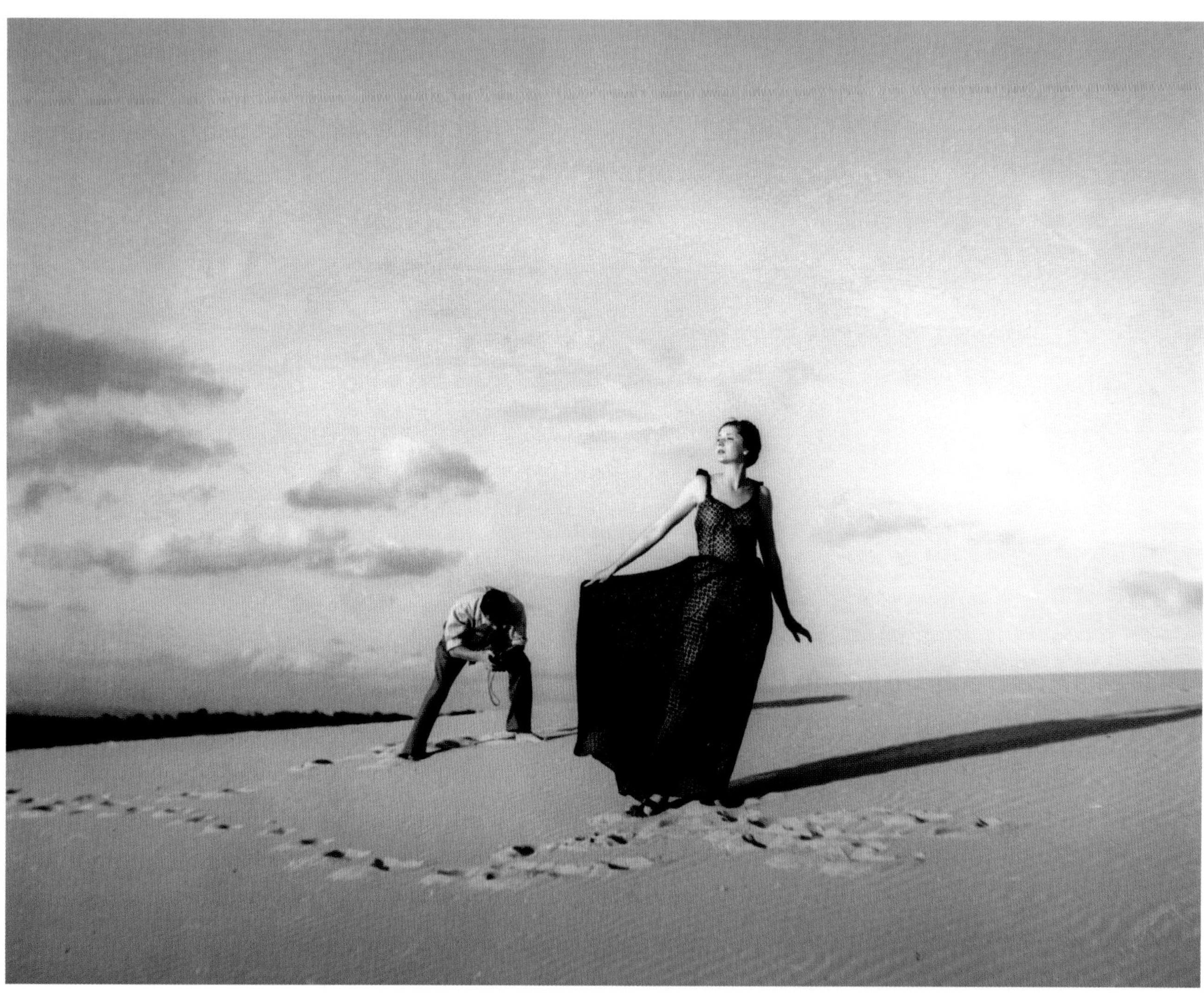

Fashion shot, Cronulla sandhills c.1937

In the late 1930s, it was becoming common practice to take fashion photographs out of doors. We would all go in Max's small car to a favourite location where he would take the required shots, my role being to help the models with their make-up and changes of costume. However, I always took my camera and would often take pictures for my own enjoyment, such as this one. Here, on sandhills at Cronulla, we see Max with his Rolleiflex photographing an evening dress for his client, David Jones. The model is Noreen Ballard, one of the best, most graceful and photogenic models who ever worked for Max. Many of our models became our friends, and are still remembered with affection.

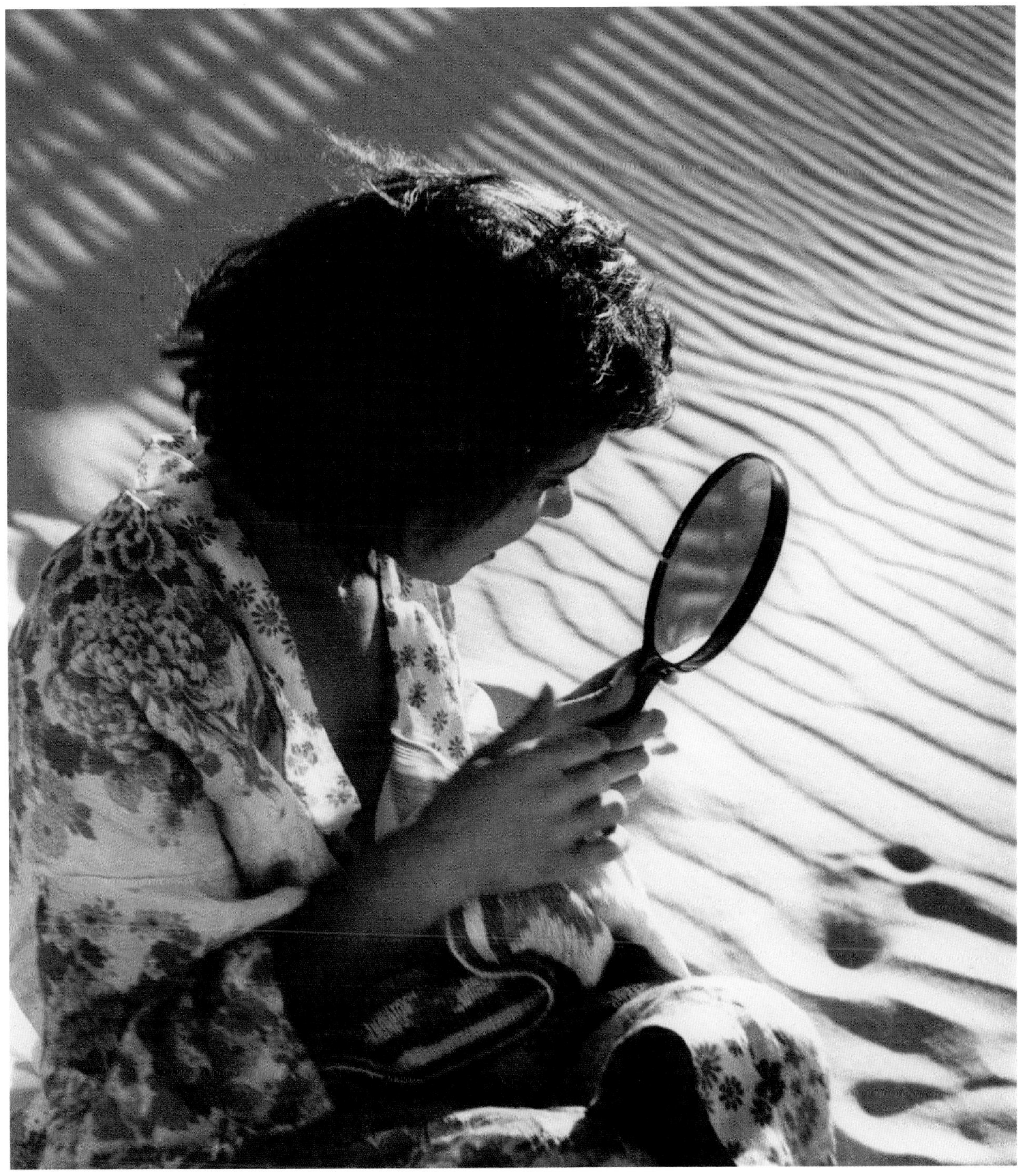

Girl with mirror 1938
The flowing lines of wind-rippled sand at Cronulla made an interesting setting for this model as she waited her turn to be photographed by Max, whose camera tripod casts the stronger long slanting lines of shadow in the top left-hand corner.

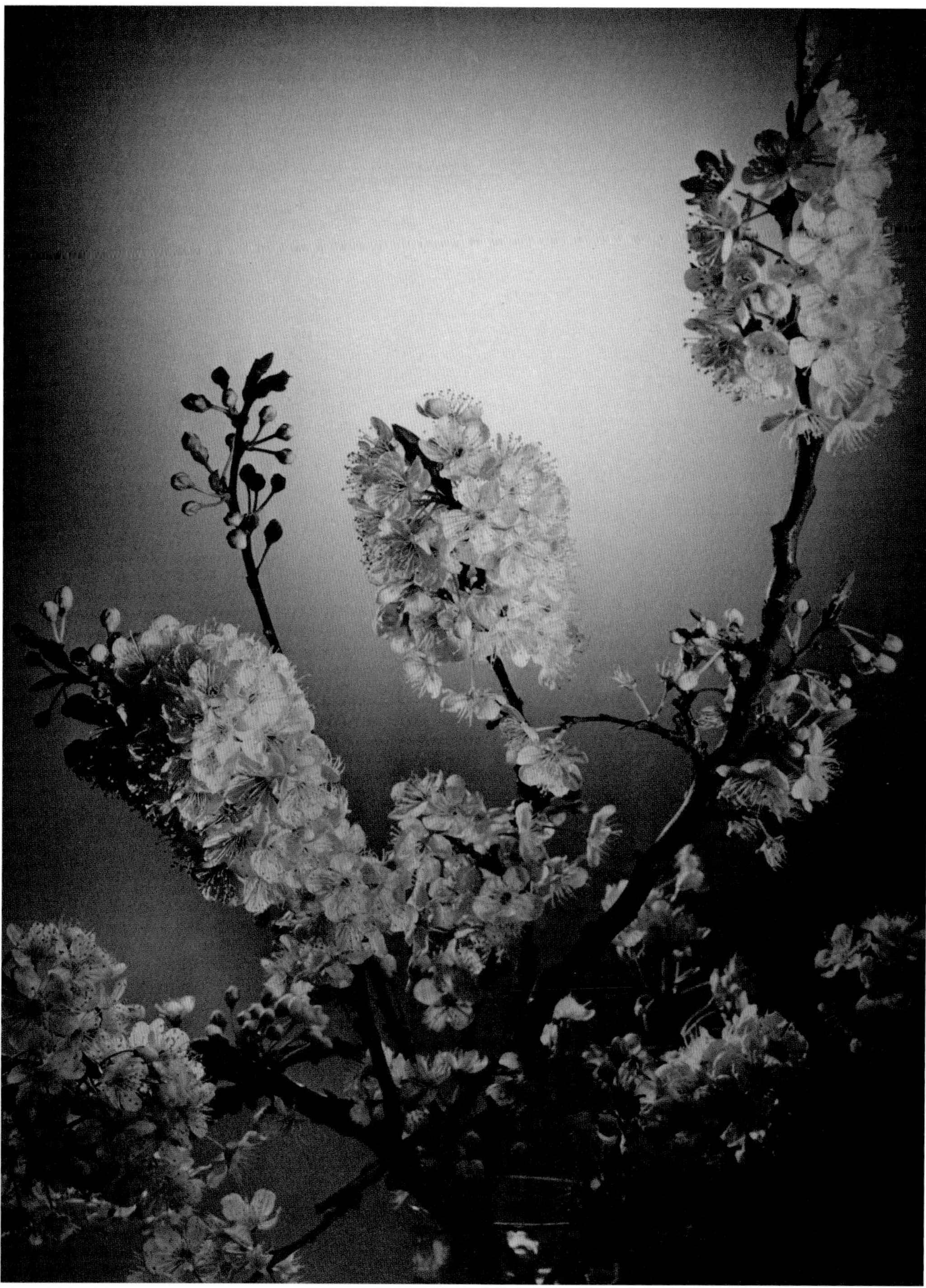

Plum blossom 1937
I photographed these beautiful heads of blossom in the studio on a large (6½ × 4½ inch) cut film negative because I wanted to bring out the petals and stamens in all their perfect detail.

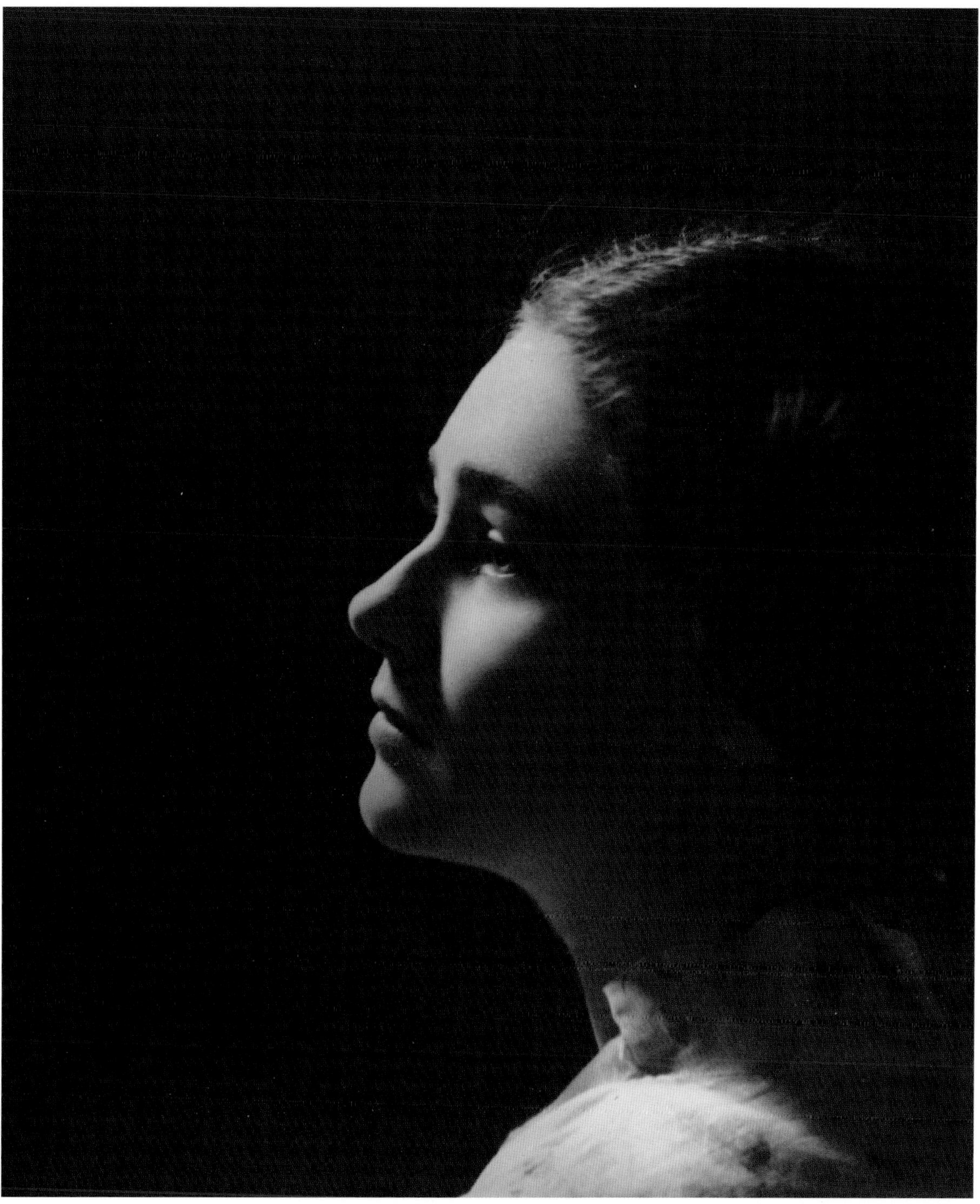

Portrait of Joyce Cotton 1938
My younger sister Joyce called in at the studio one day, and I decided to take her portrait impromptu. I felt that simple lighting and a dark background was appropriate, to hold the viewer's interest on her face and her unselfconscious expression.

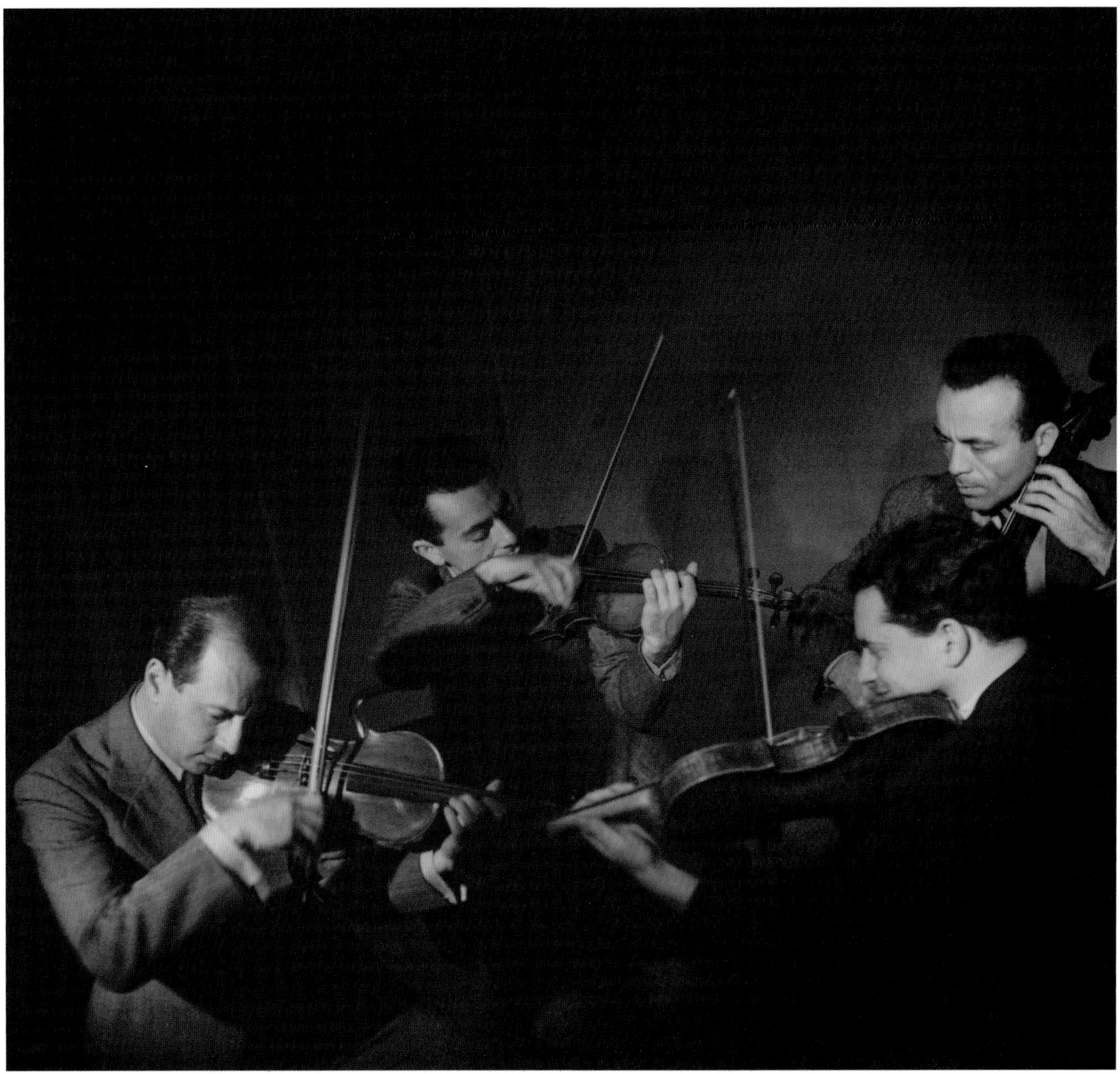

The Budapest String Quartet c.1937

[National Gallery of Australia]

This quartet was sent to Max's studio for publicity photographs to help promote their series of concerts. While Max was arranging them for their official photograph, I wandered about them with my Rolleiflex looking for interesting viewpoints.

And then they began a serenade by Tchaikovsky. This was an exciting moment and I decided to get a shot of them actually playing. This did not constrain me to show all their faces clearly as for a publicity shot. I wanted to get the feeling of a group making music that they loved—I think the violinist on the left-hand side of the picture best shows this.

I went to several of their concerts in the Sydney Conservatorium of Music. I sat by myself near the front of the audience, absolutely rapt in their music, and was in seventh heaven when the cellist actually smiled at me while playing. I still hear the opening bars of the serenade when I look at this photograph.

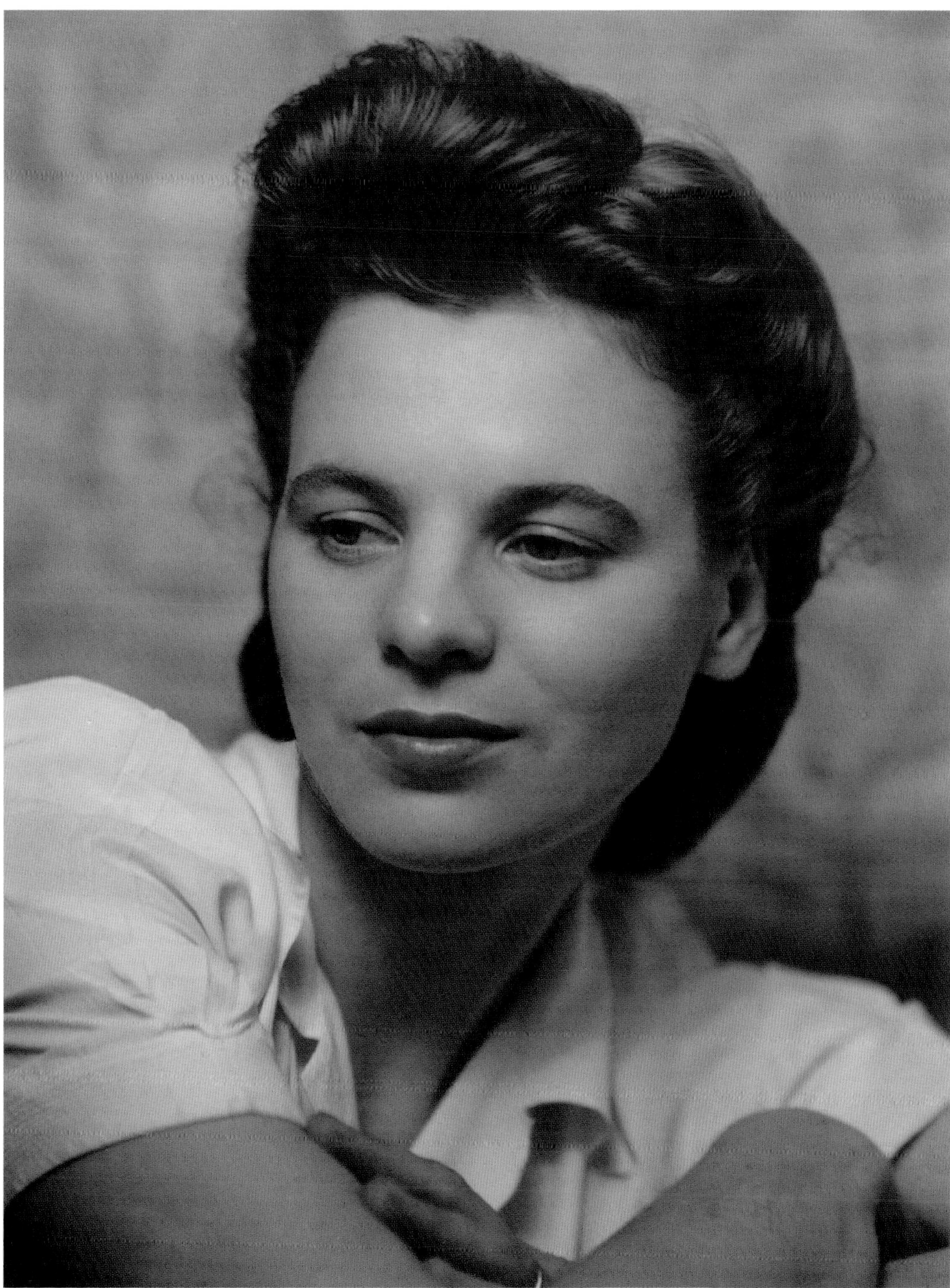

Portrait by candlelight 1943

For a long time I had wanted to take a portrait by the light of one candle, thinking that its gentle luminosity and soft shadows would be ideal for that purpose. I asked Jean Lorraine if she would come to the studio after work, and we waited until daylight was gone so that we could have complete darkness. I used the studio portrait camera, which had a shutter controlled by pressure on a squeeze-bulb, attached to the camera by a long thin piece of rubber.

Jean took a relaxed pose, which she would be able to hold comfortably, and then with all the lights out I lit a candle. With one hand holding it aloft and the other gripping the squeeze-bulb, I opened the shutter to expose the film for a carefully calculated ninety seconds. (I knew the strength in candlepower of the lights and had calculated the exposure needed.) Jean was the ideal person for this experiment—she did not make the slightest movement and we were both pleased with the result.

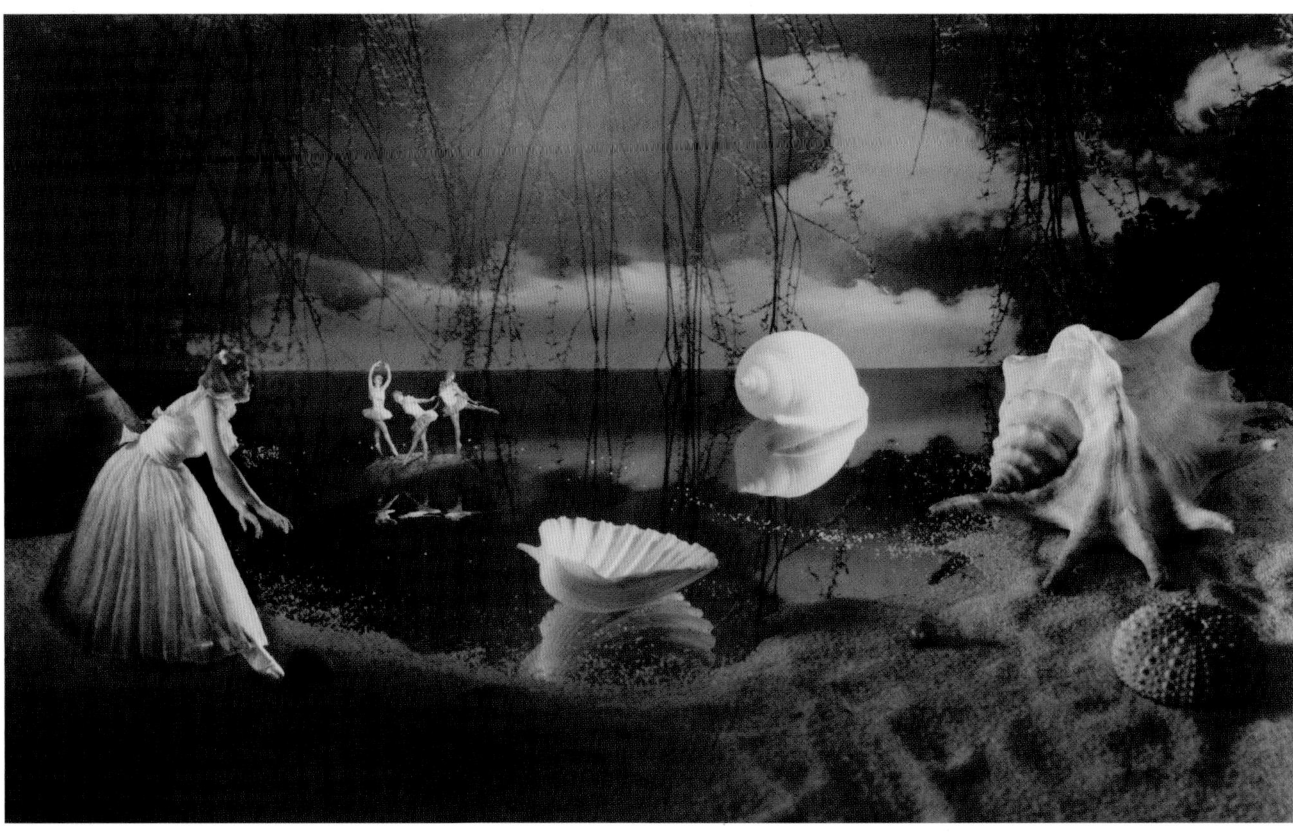

Theme for a mural 1942

During the war, though Max and I had separated amicably in 1941 and I had gone to teach mathematics at Frensham School in Mittagong, Max and his business associate Ernest Hyde asked me to come back and run the studio (single-handed) while they were enlisted in the services, which I was very happy to do. One of my commissions came from a Sydney architect, Sam Lipson, to design and produce a photographic mural 6 feet long and 2½ feet high, for one of his clients. The only other stipulation was that it should contain ballet dancers.

I engaged a charming young model who was also a ballet dancer to come and pose for me, with two changes of costume. I took many shots of her in various traditional ballet poses, from which I chose four. Then I had to devise an appropriate setting for the dancers. I wanted to give a sense of depth to my picture. Eventually I made a large negative of willow streamers reflected in a highly polished stainless steel sheet with a miniature setting of stones, sand and shells in the foreground. I made a second large negative with the dancers reduced to a suitable scale, set in a clear film background, and then put these two together to make the final composite negative. One of the images was reversed, since I put the sensitised sides of the negatives together for maximum sharpness.

The 6 feet of photographic paper was obtained in one roll, and I enlisted someone to help me pull it to and fro through the chemicals in a very large wooden dish on the darkroom floor. We rolled and unrolled it through baths of developer, water, hypo and more water. Then my helper went home and the print was transferred to more water in the long darkroom sink. It had to be thoroughly washed (there was no hypo clearing agent in those days), so I stayed all night at the studio to change the water in the sink every hour.

The print reproduced here is made from the whole composite negative. Long and narrow proportions were required for the client's print, so that only a central horizontal section of the negative was used, but it contained all the necessary elements. Recently I heard that it had been stripped off the wall (somewhere in the eastern suburbs of Sydney) only a few years ago, so it lasted well for over forty years.

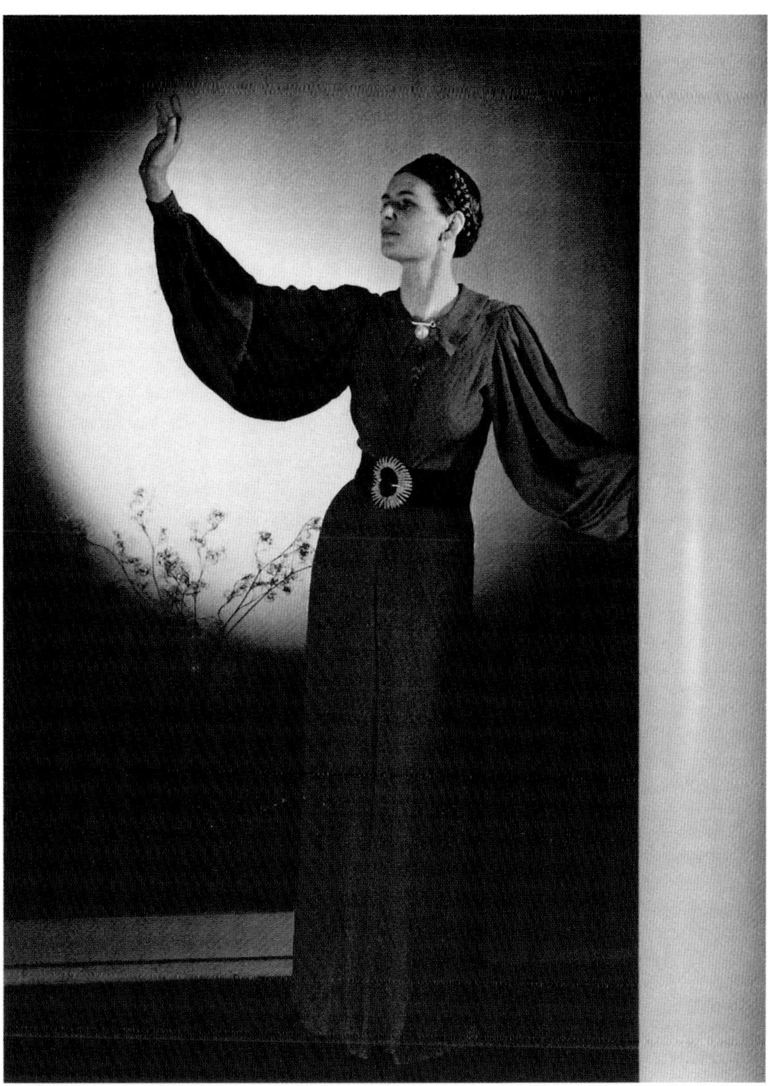

Gwynneth Stone 1942

Gwen, as we called her, was an artist and dress designer. She was slim and graceful, with great poise and serenity. I enjoyed taking her portrait. Forty-eight years later, a friend showed me a recently taken snapshot of her, still with a wonderful face full of character and repose. Ageing need hold no fears with such an example as hers to look upon.

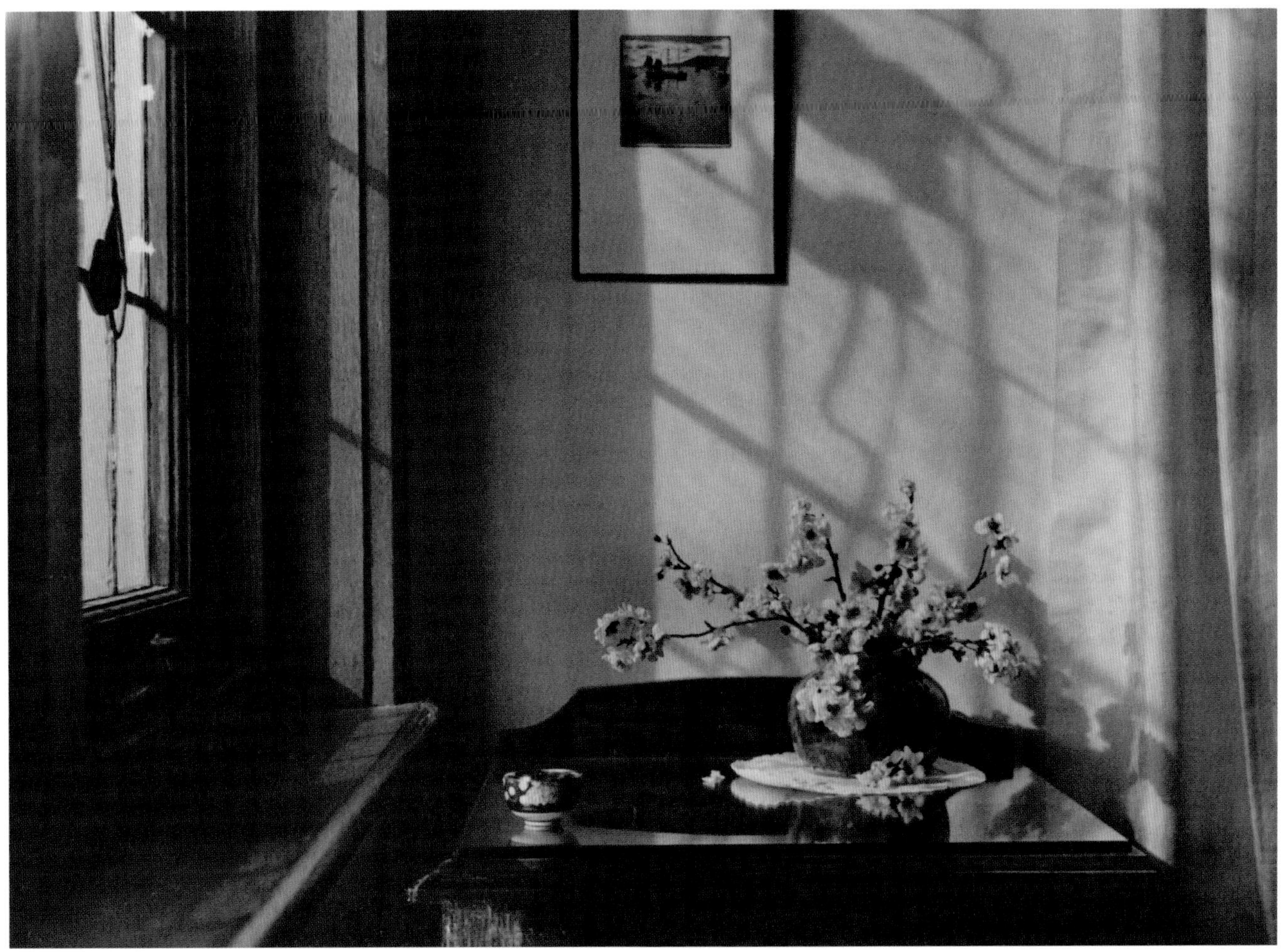

Interior c.1926

[National Gallery of Australia]

My family lived in a large house overlooking a valley of unspoilt bushland at Hornsby. When we were young my sister Joyce and I shared this room. Its stained-glass windows had a simple floral motif which cast attractive shadows on the wall in the lace afternoon.

Under the house there was space for a small darkroom. The house had high foundations and was built on a huge level shelf of natural rock; my darkroom workbench was part of this rock. My father improvised an enlarger and taught me how to develop my films and prints, explaining the scientific principles of cameras and chemicals as he did so. He had learnt the principles of photography so that he could take pictures at the Antarctic during a six-week round trip he made there (as a young scientist and crew member of the little *Nimrod*) with Shackleton's expedition of 1907–09. The then Professor of Geology at Sydney University, Edgeworth David, was also a member of the party; he and my father were good friends and colleagues. When Edgeworth David retired in 1924, my father succeeded him as Professor of Geology.

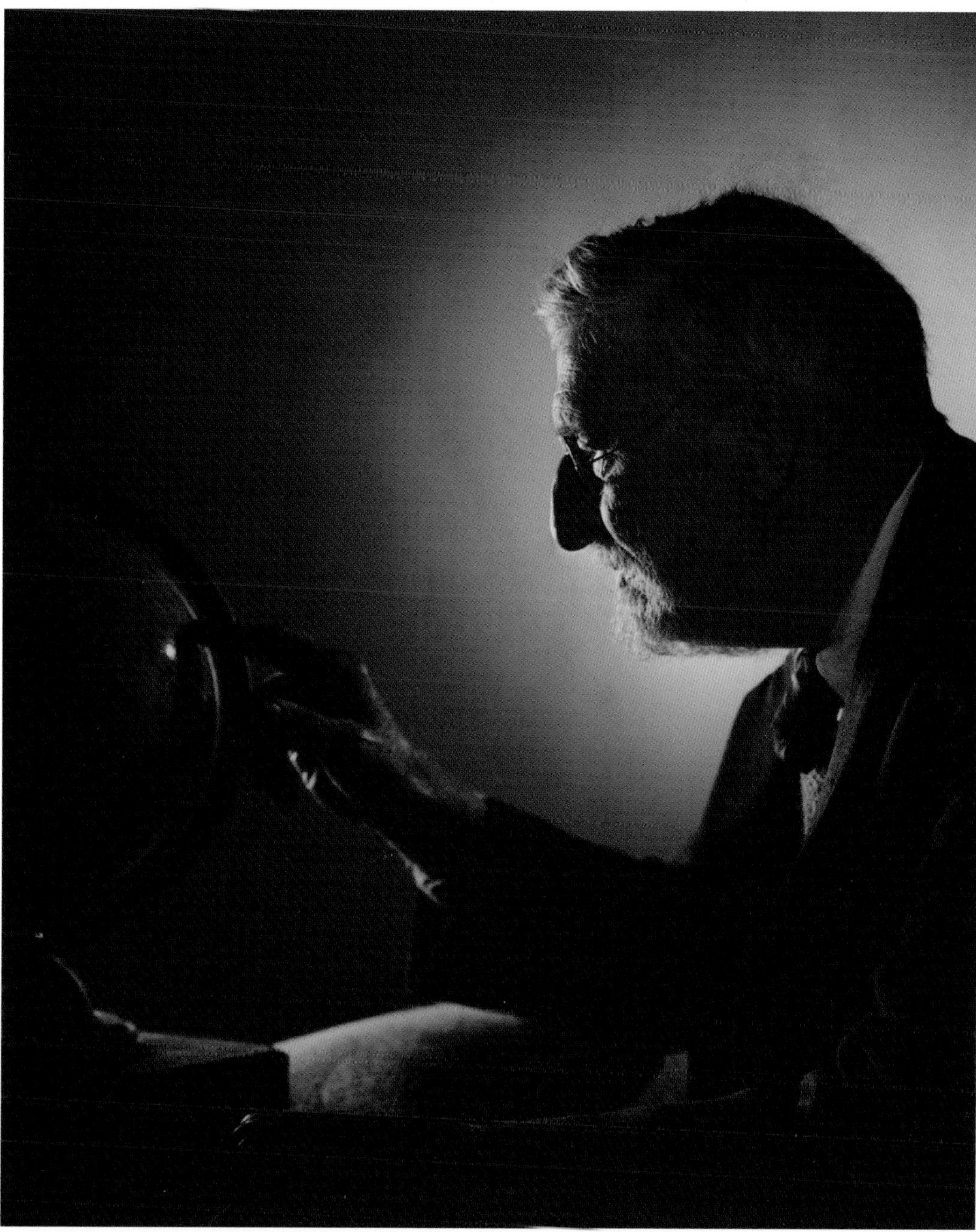

My grandfather, Frank Cotton c.1935

When I had reached the age of twelve or so, I often used to call on my grandfather and grandmother Cotton in the afternoon after Sunday School. They lived nearby and always made me welcome. I have many memories of sitting on the edge of their back verandah and listening to my grandfather talk of the days when he was prospecting, droving, sleeper-cutting, writing articles for *The World's News*, and of the time later on when he became a member of the first Labor caucus. My grandfather christened one of his sons 'Karl Marx' Cotton, although that child later changed his name to the non-political 'Max'.

Later, when my grandfather was in his seventies, I persuaded him to come to Max Dupain's studio, as I wanted to take his portrait. He lived at North Sydney then, and always walked over the Harbour Bridge when visiting the city.

In this photograph I suspect that he is pointing to Russia on the globe, as he was keen to know how the Five Year Plan was working out—he wholeheartedly approved of the idealism then embodied in Russian socialism, and used to quote 'From each according to his ability, to each according to his needs'.

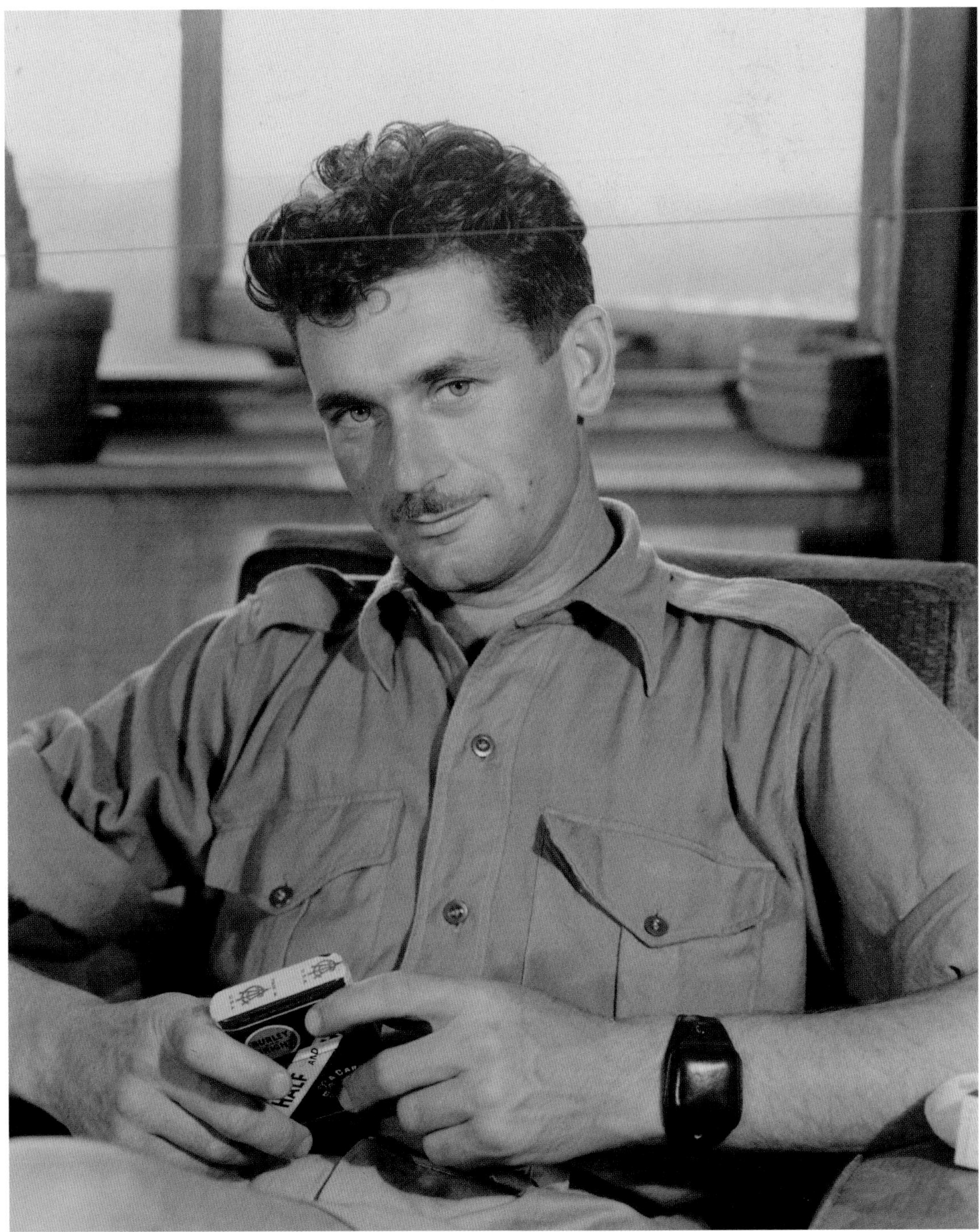

Ross McInerney 1942

[National Gallery of Australia, gift of the artist 1987]

Jean Lorraine, who had become one of my closest friends, married Dr John McInerney, and through her I met her husband's parents, his five younger brothers and little sister, Haidee. Ross, the second-oldest brother, called in to the studio on brief leave from the army training camp at Bonegilla, and I suggested that I should take his photograph just as he sat there at the window, to give to his parents. After that we saw more of each other whenever possible during the war years, and we married about two-and-a-half years later.

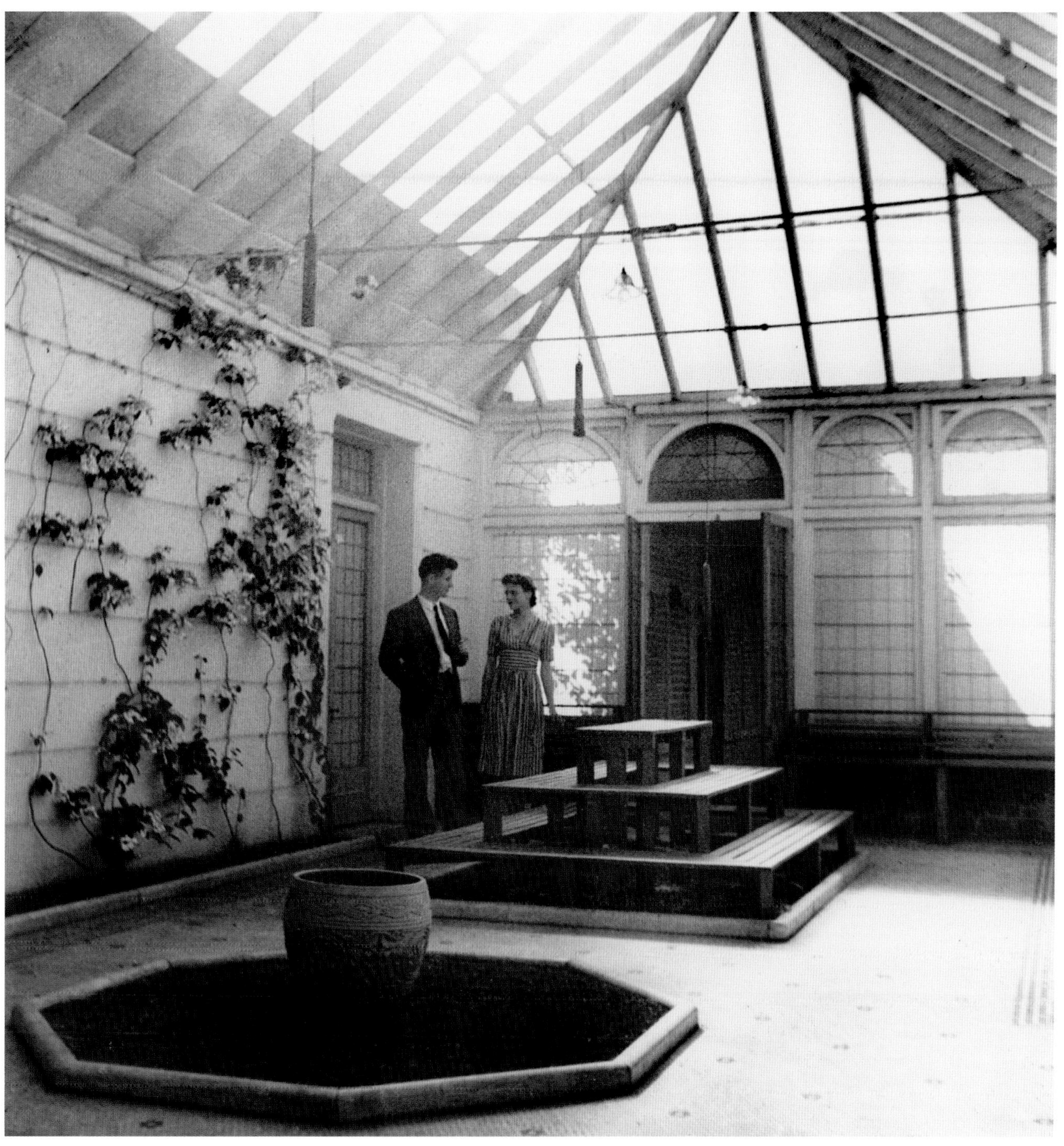

The Conservatory at Yaralla c.1941

John McInerney, recently graduated from medical school at Sydney University, suggested that I might like to take some photographs of the grounds at Yaralla Hospital at Concord. This conservatory (since demolished) was part of the hospital estate, formerly the home of Dame Eadith Walker, who had bequeathed it to the New South Wales government to be used as a convalescent home for returned servicemen.

The conservatory must have been a very pleasant place. One can imagine it full of exotic plants flourishing in natural light gently diffused by the glass roof, but here the building is empty except for a creeper on the wall, and the figures of John McInerney and Jean Lorraine.

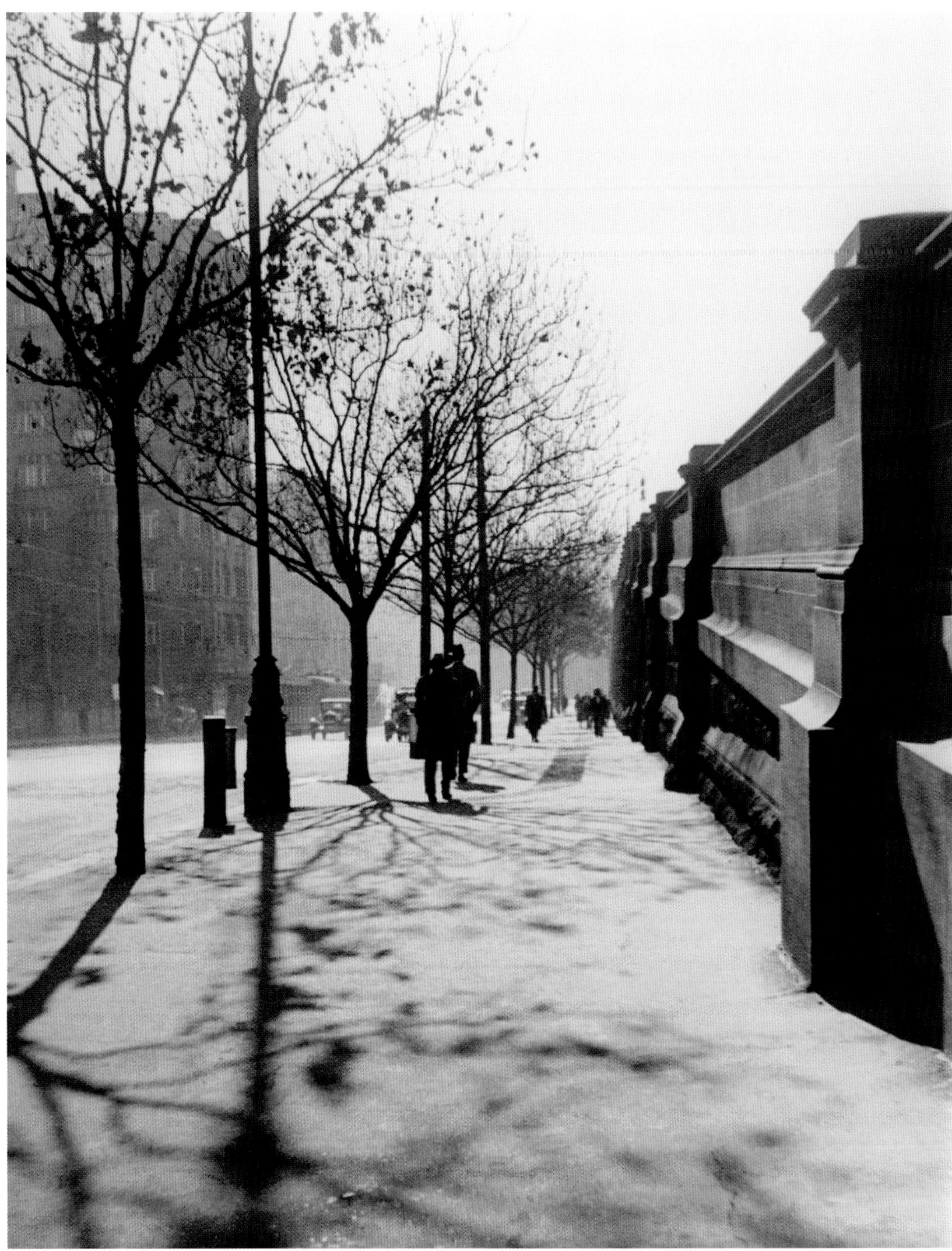

Pitt Street, Sydney c.1930
I rook this view of Pitt Street after walking down from Central Railway Station. The autumn light was clear and cast a pattern of tree shadows on the footpath; the stone wall added strength and the small figures gave life to the whole scene.

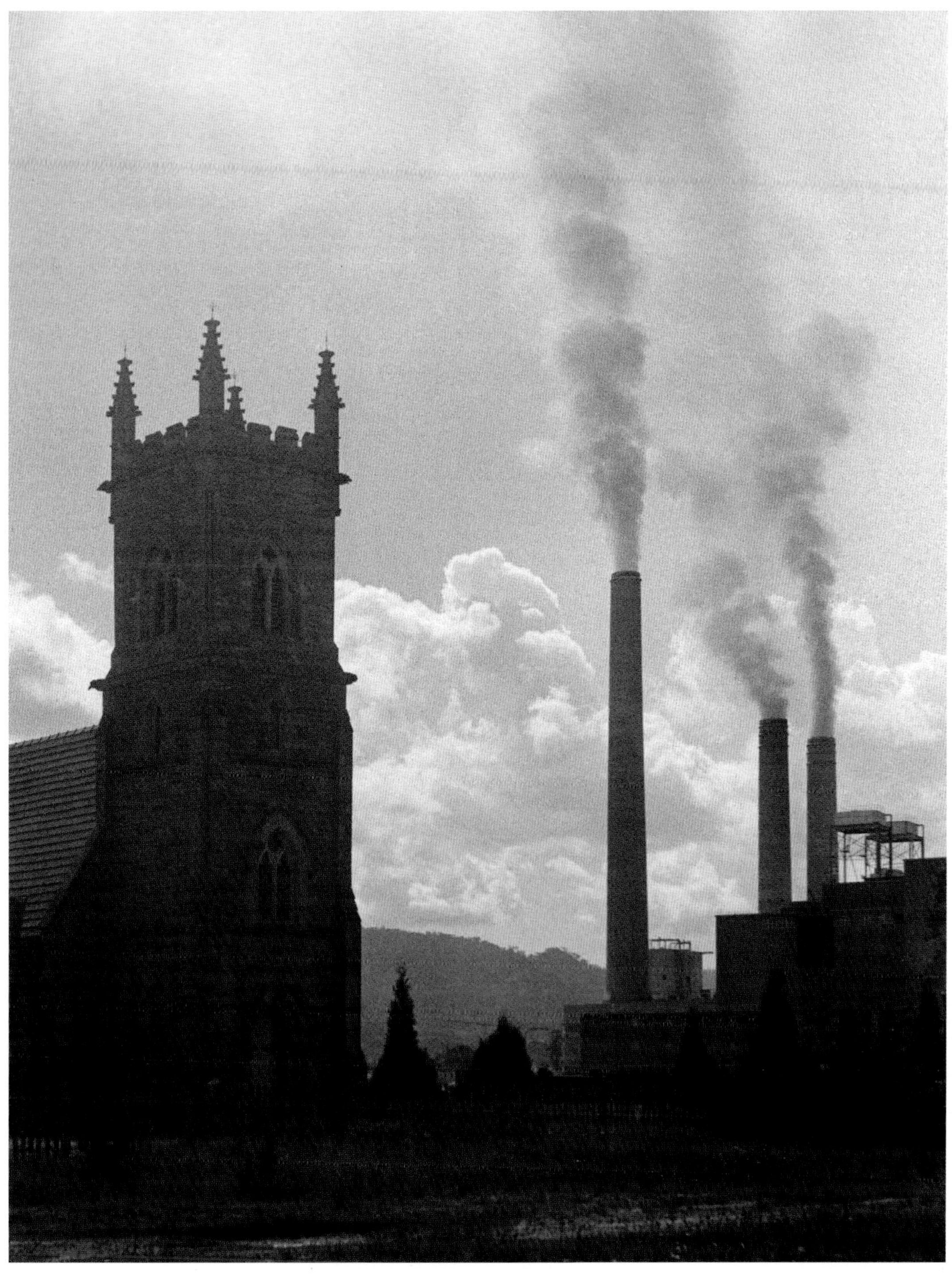

Power house, Wallerawang 1964
The pure vertical lines of the slender power house chimneys with their rising smoke were balanced by the dark bulk of the church, making a satisfying composition and conveying a gentle mood of evening.

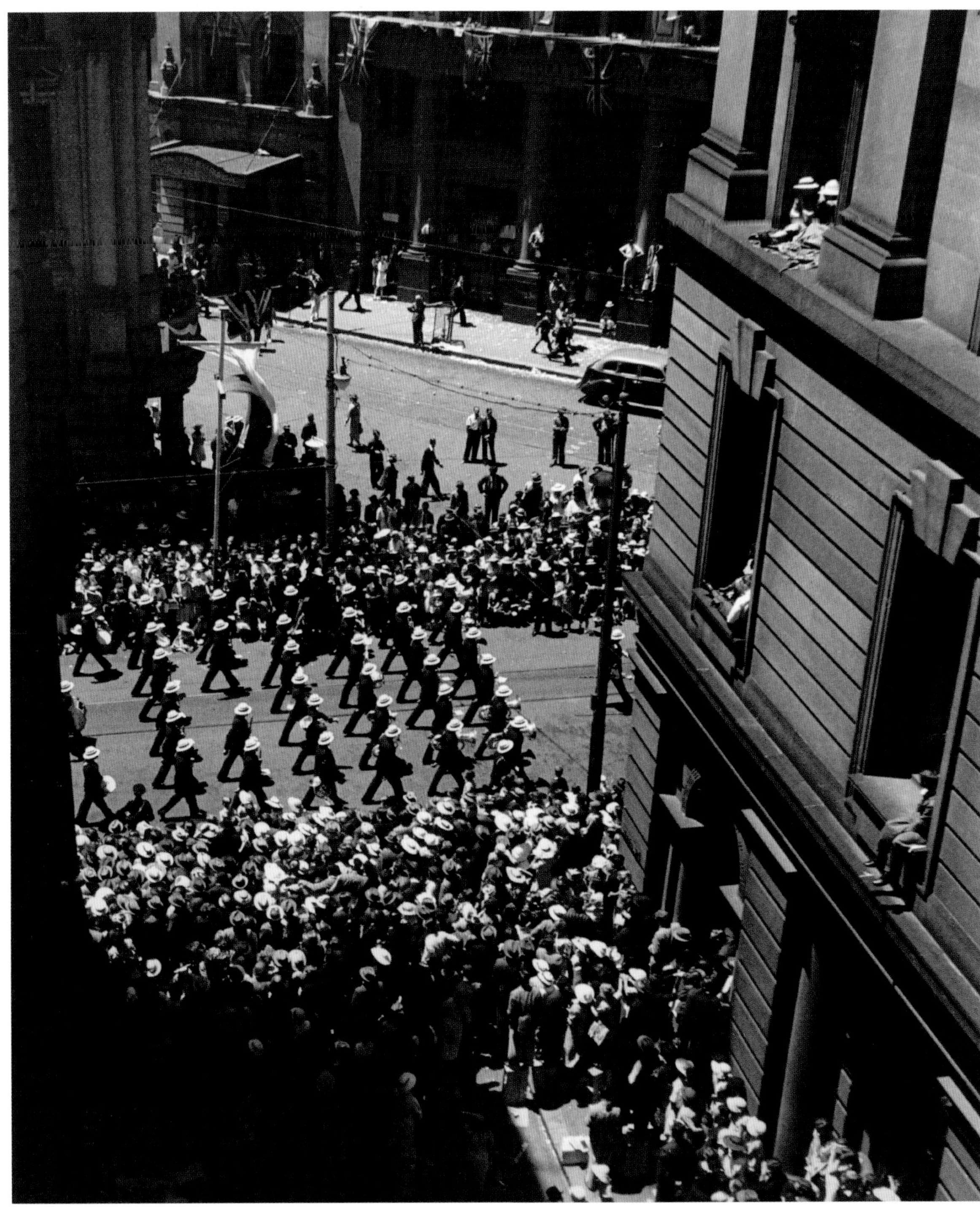

Sesquicentenary procession, Sydney 1938
From a high window in a city building I photographed several groups as they were passing in procession, and chose this shot because I liked all the neat triangles formed by the legs of the marchers and the street surface.

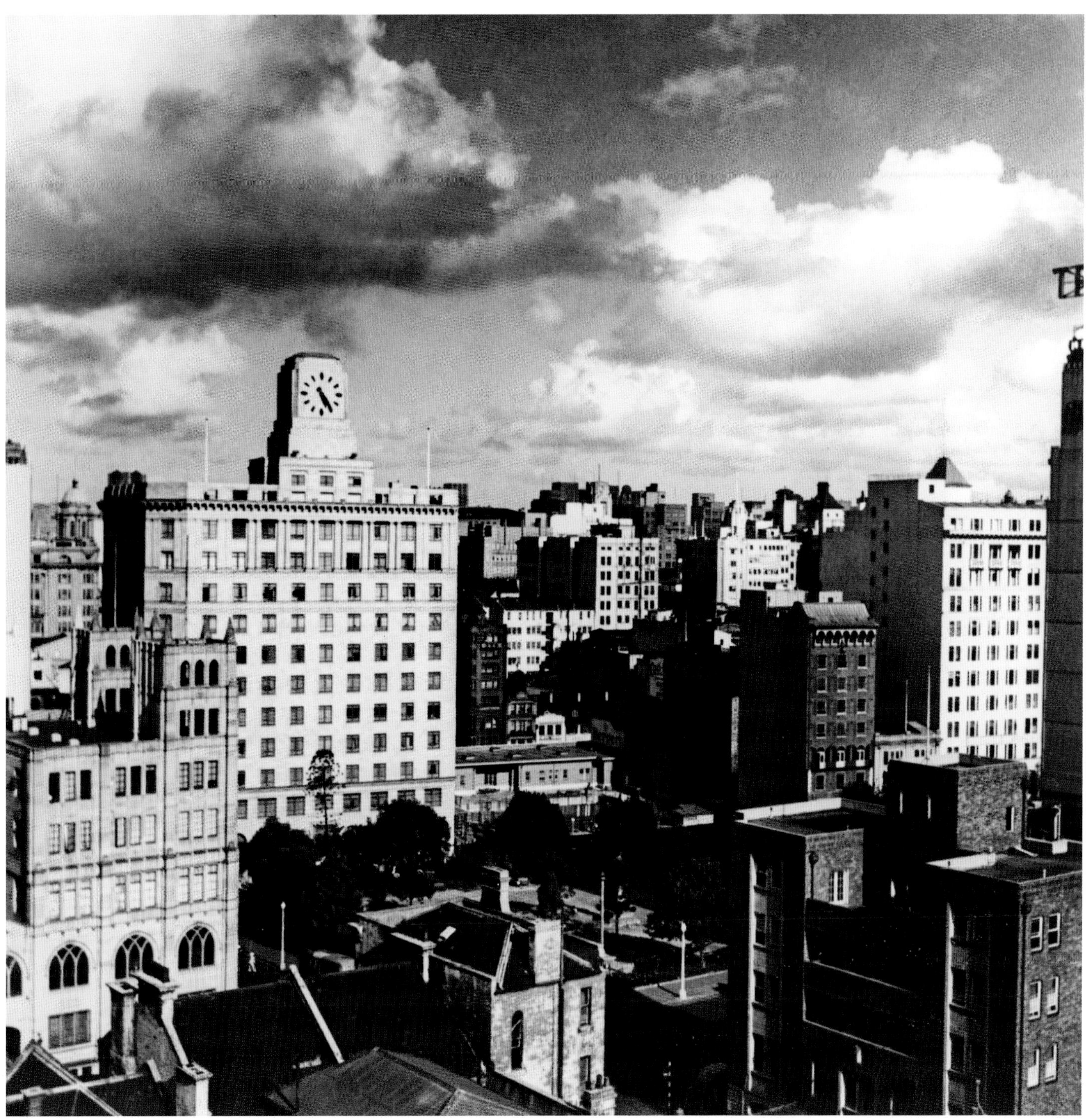

City view from 49 *Clarence Street* c.1942
Through the window of Max's Sydney studio at 49 Clarence Street (since demolished) I noticed that a wonderful sky was building up, and hurried to the rooftop with my camera.

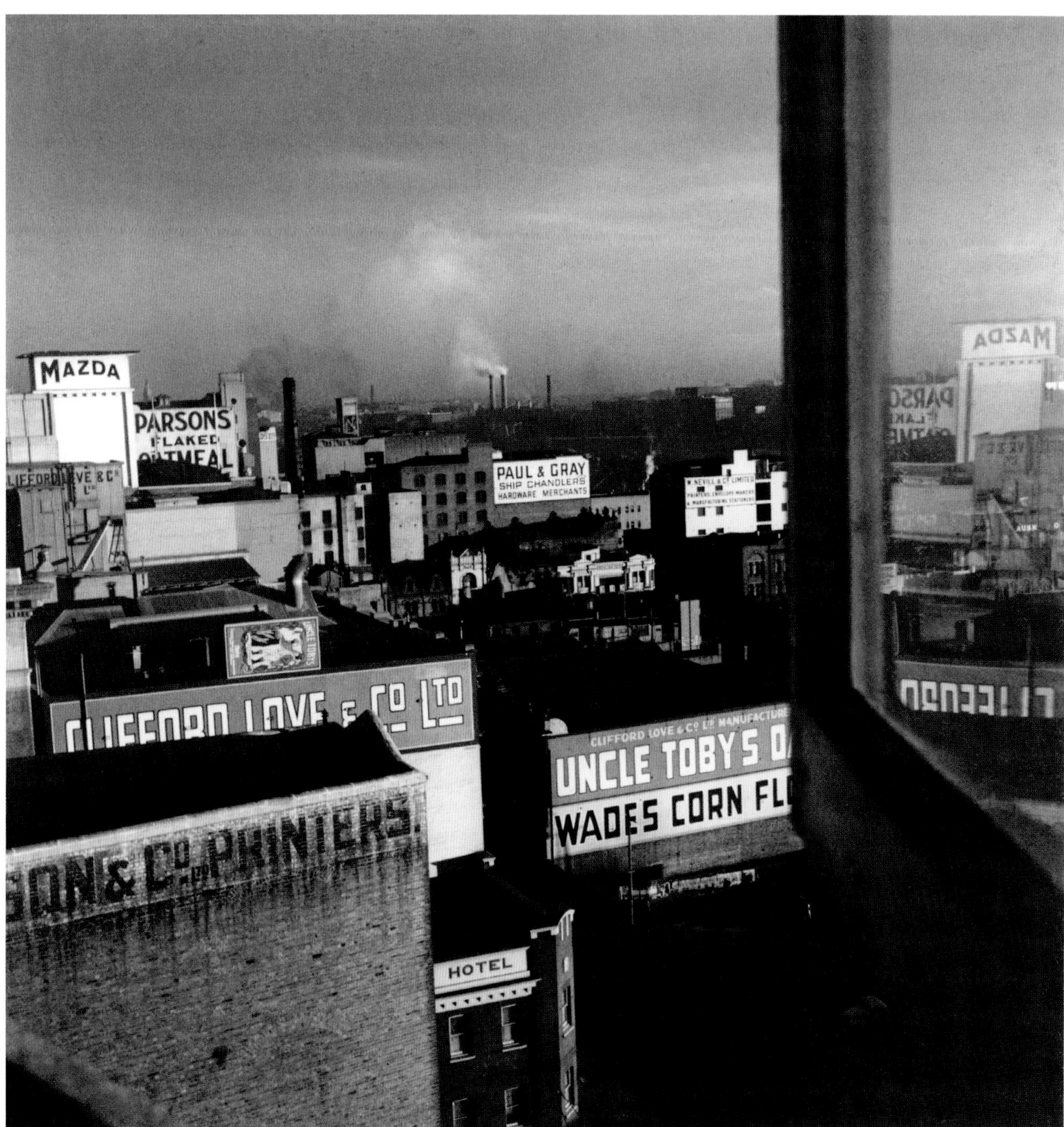

City rooftops 1942
This view was taken from a studio window at 49 Clarence Street, looking down the street towards the Town Hall. The low sun shining on the rooftops accentuated all the vertical signs, including my favourite, Uncle Toby's Oats, lying on its side.

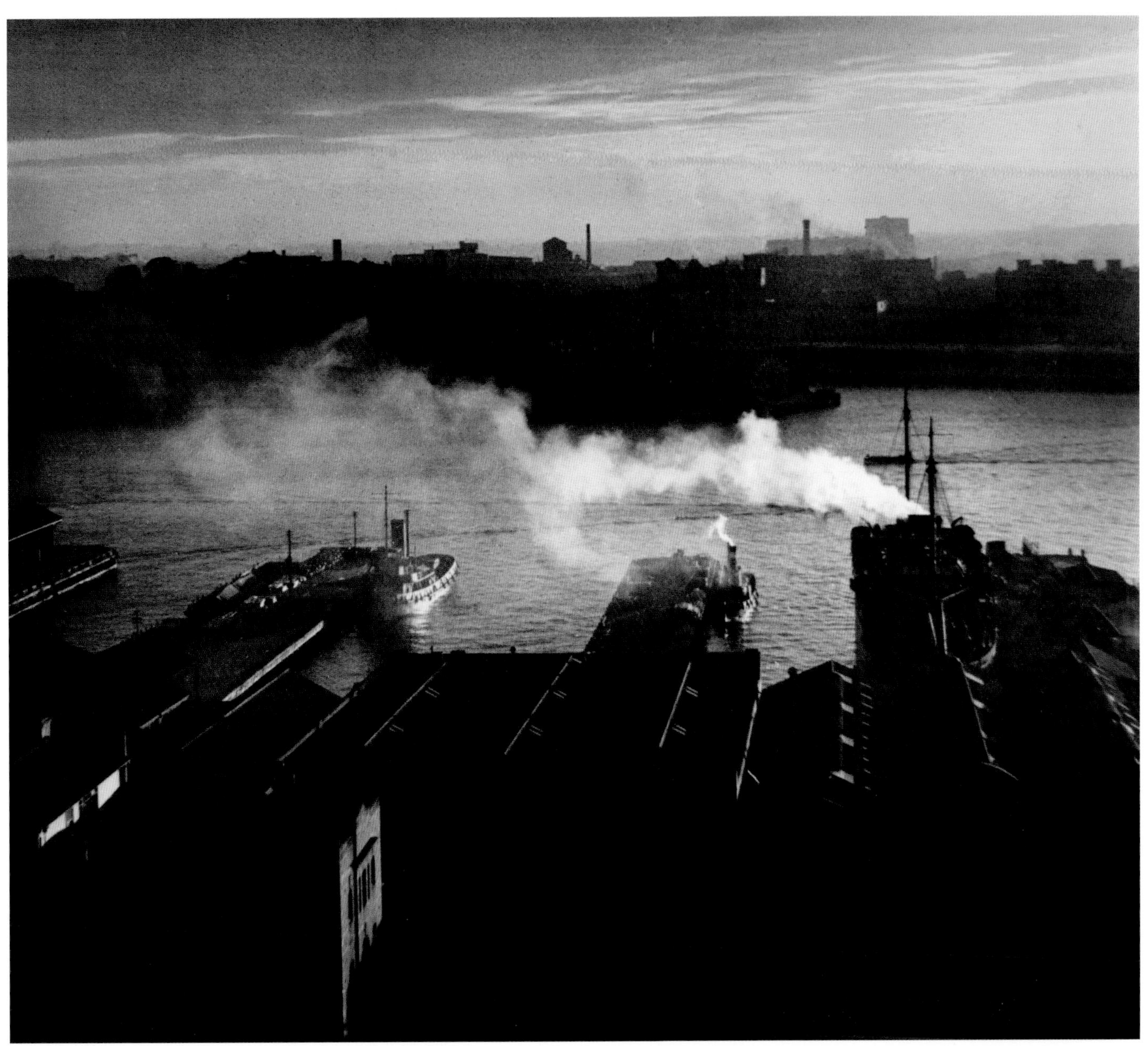

Darling Harbour c.1942
This photograph was also taken from Max's studio at 49 Clarence Street. The windows were tall and wide, and from them one had an unbroken view of the harbour and wharves. I became very fond of this view. There was always something happening on the waterfront; and one day during the war years I watched the Australian hospital ship *Manunda* slowly coming down the harbour, unannounced, and knew that a friend of ours, the artist Richard Beck, a member of its medical unit, was safely back from the war zone—this time, at least.

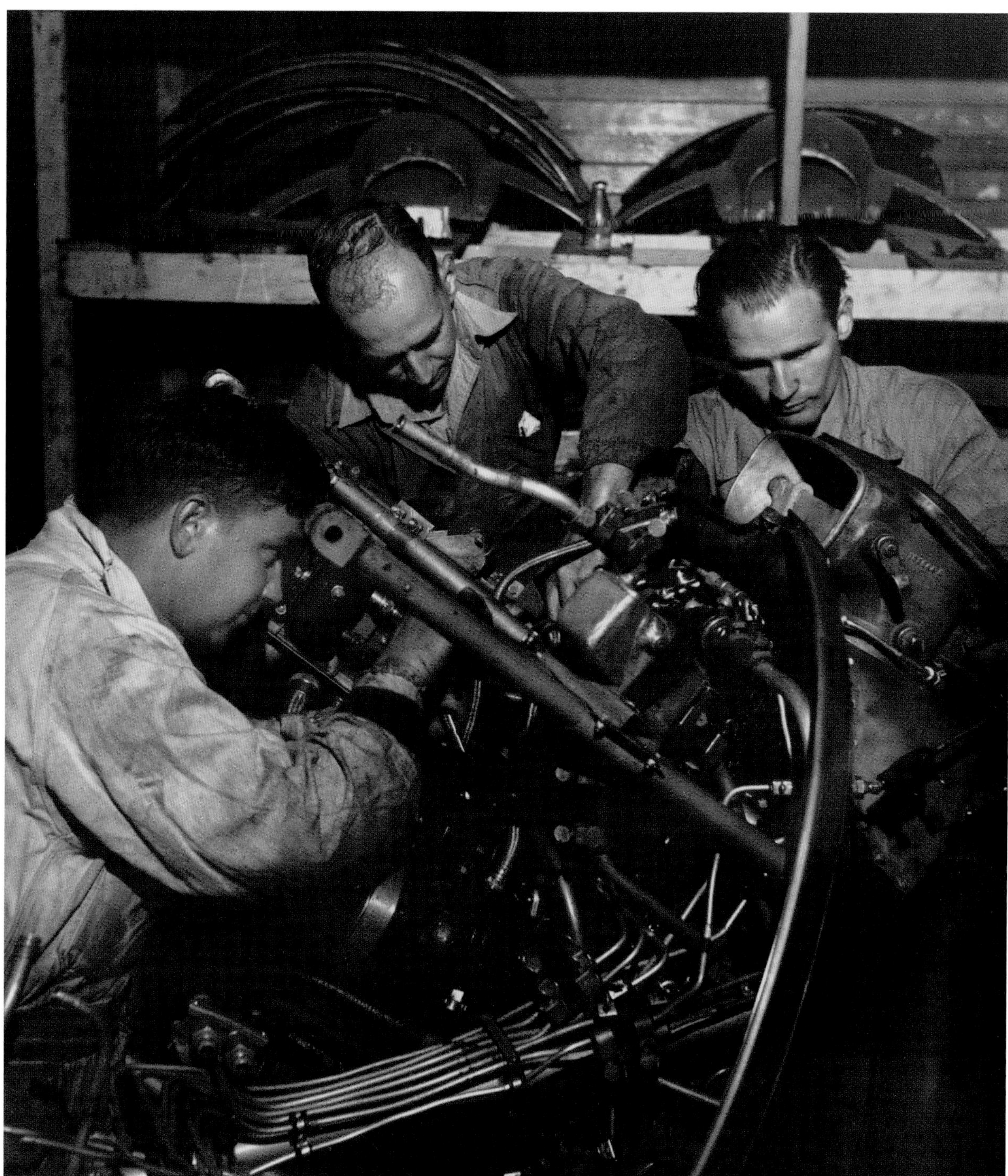

Aircraft mechanics 1945

[National Gallery of Australia]

This study of workers in de Havilland's aircraft factory was commissioned for publication in a book about the Air Force, called *Wings of Tomorrow*. I liked the circular composition—as if the men, concentrating on their work, were swept up in the workings of the complicated machinery.

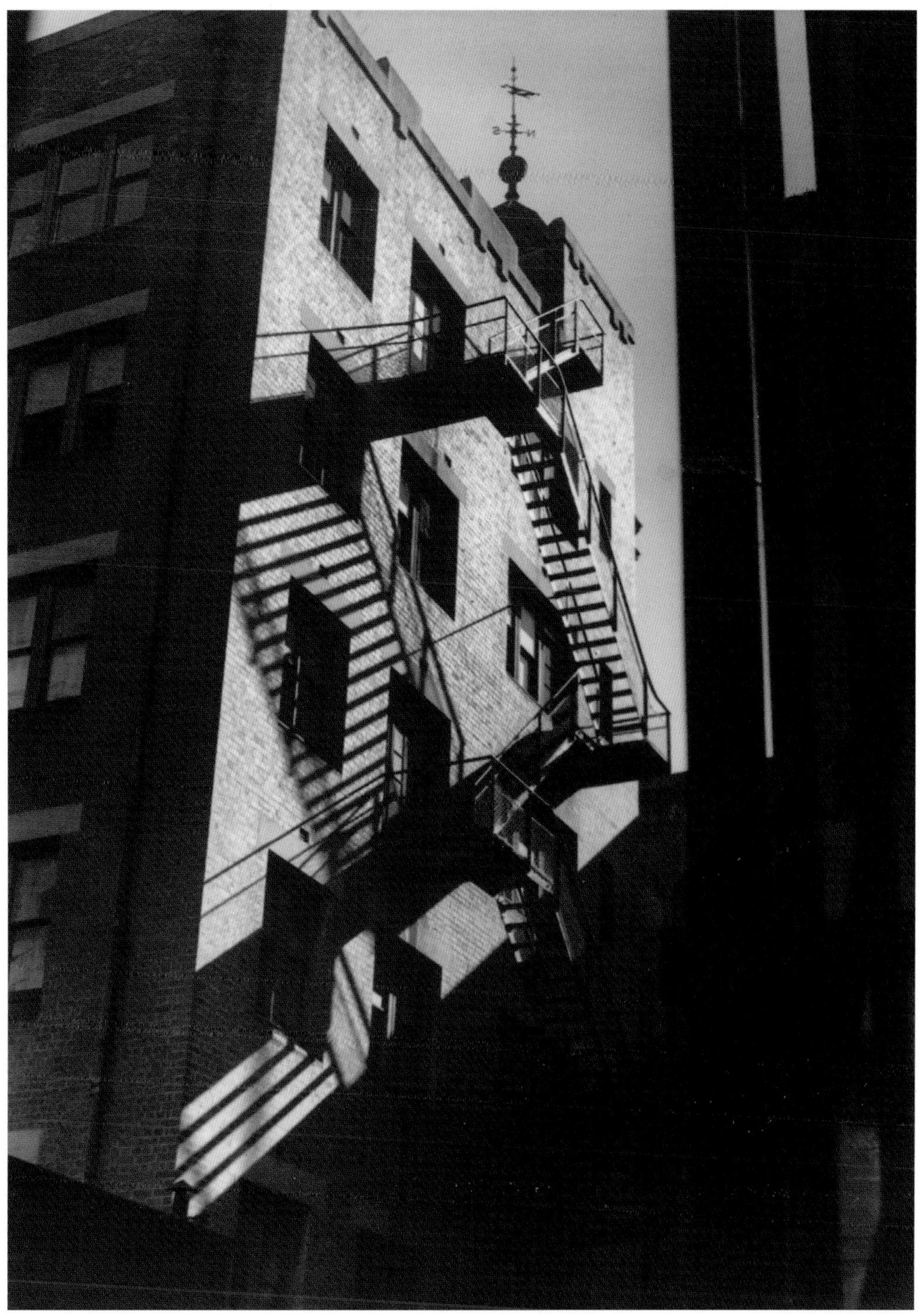

Fire escape c.1935
I was fond of looking out of windows. This was taken from a back window in Max's first studio in Bond Street. The sun was casting a shadow that was a faithful repetition of the metal staircase's sharp, clean lines, but the shadow was enlarged on the wall and appeared much stronger than the staircase itself.

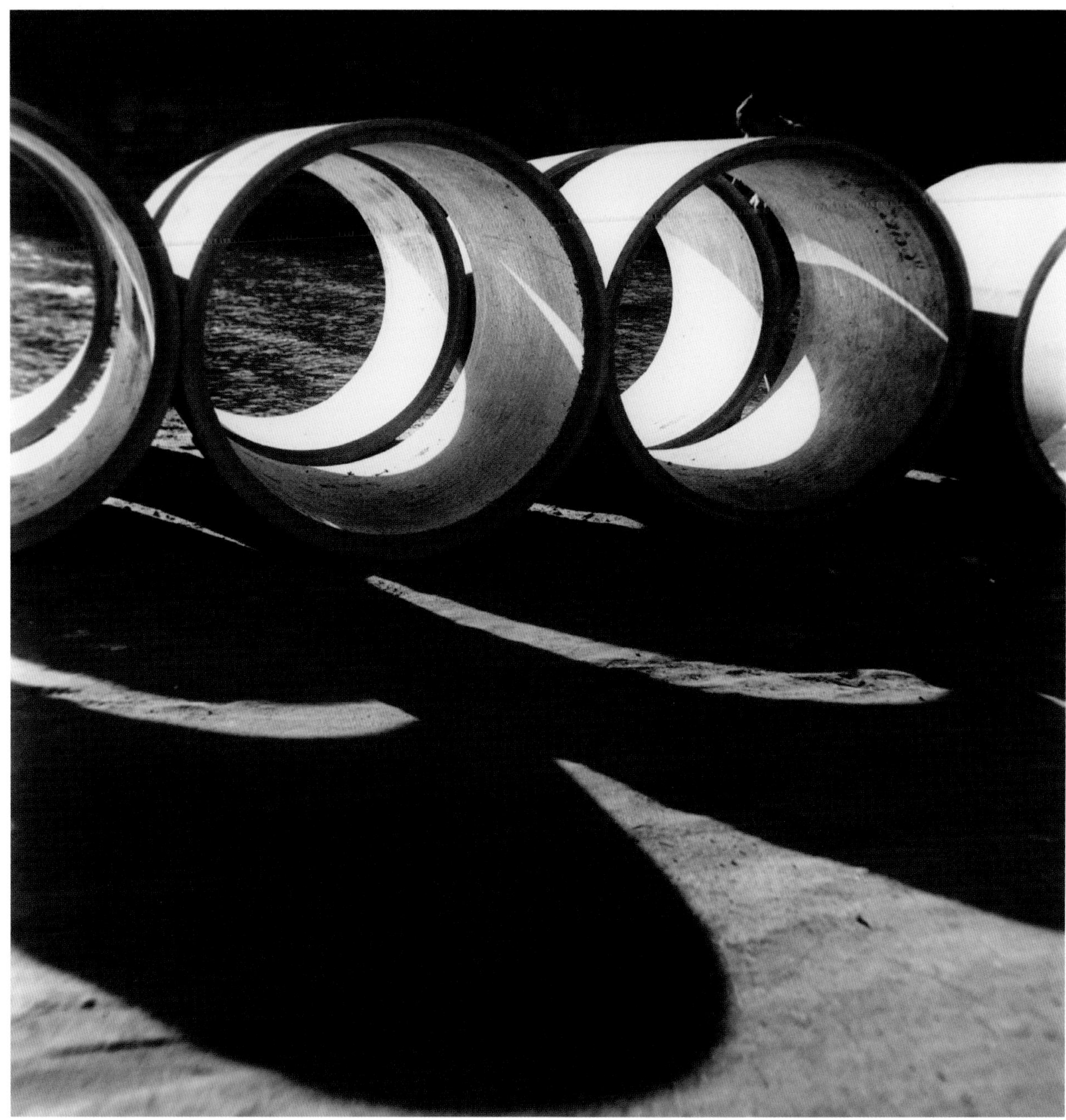

Drainpipes 1937

When I saw these drainpipes I was impressed with their shapes and shadows. There was a suggestion of geometrical precision in their circles and curves, interspersed with slivers of light.

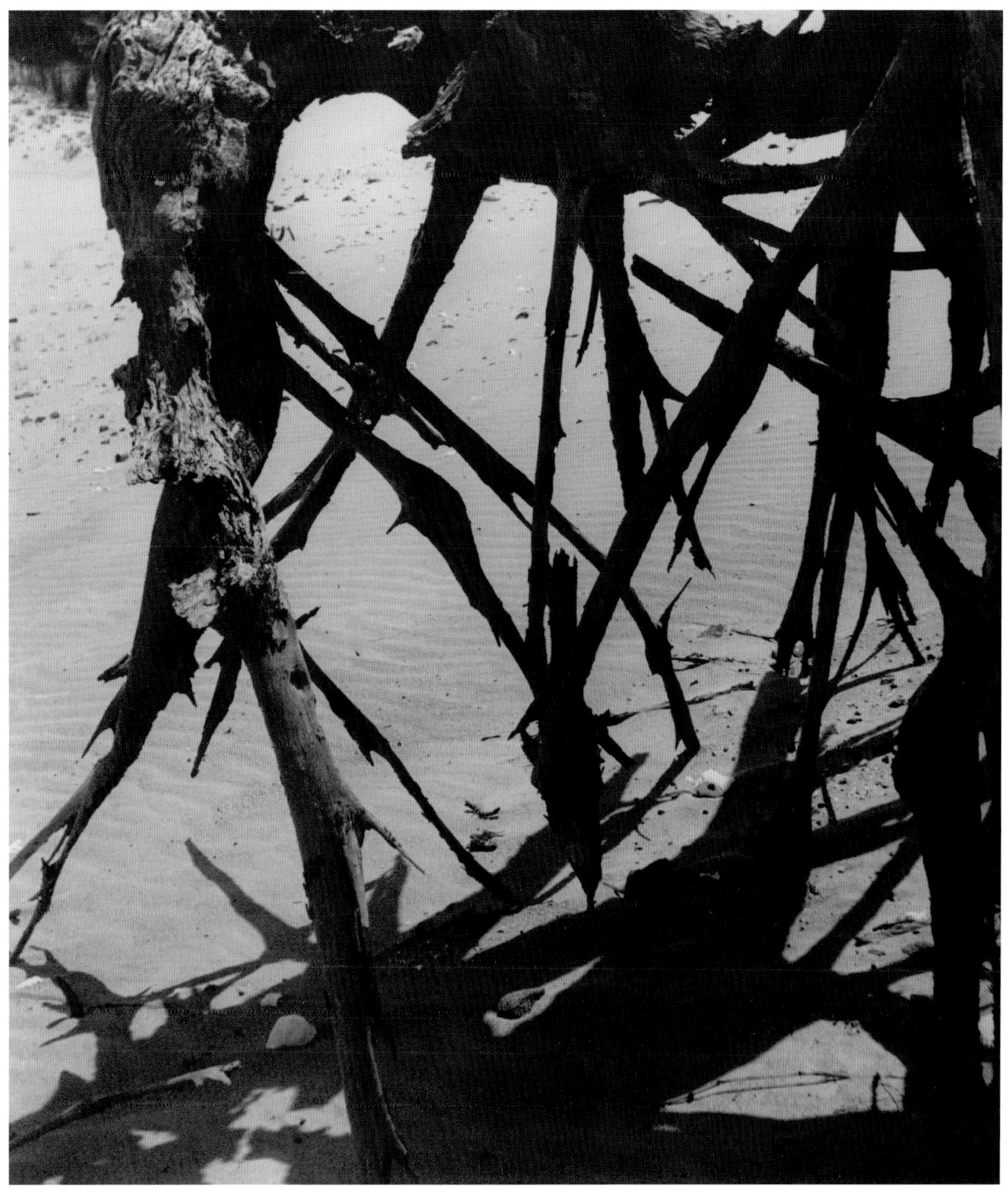

Driftwood c.1960
I noticed this driftwood cast up on the beach at Newport during the Christmas holidays, in strange shapes like a gathering of compasses marking out the sand.

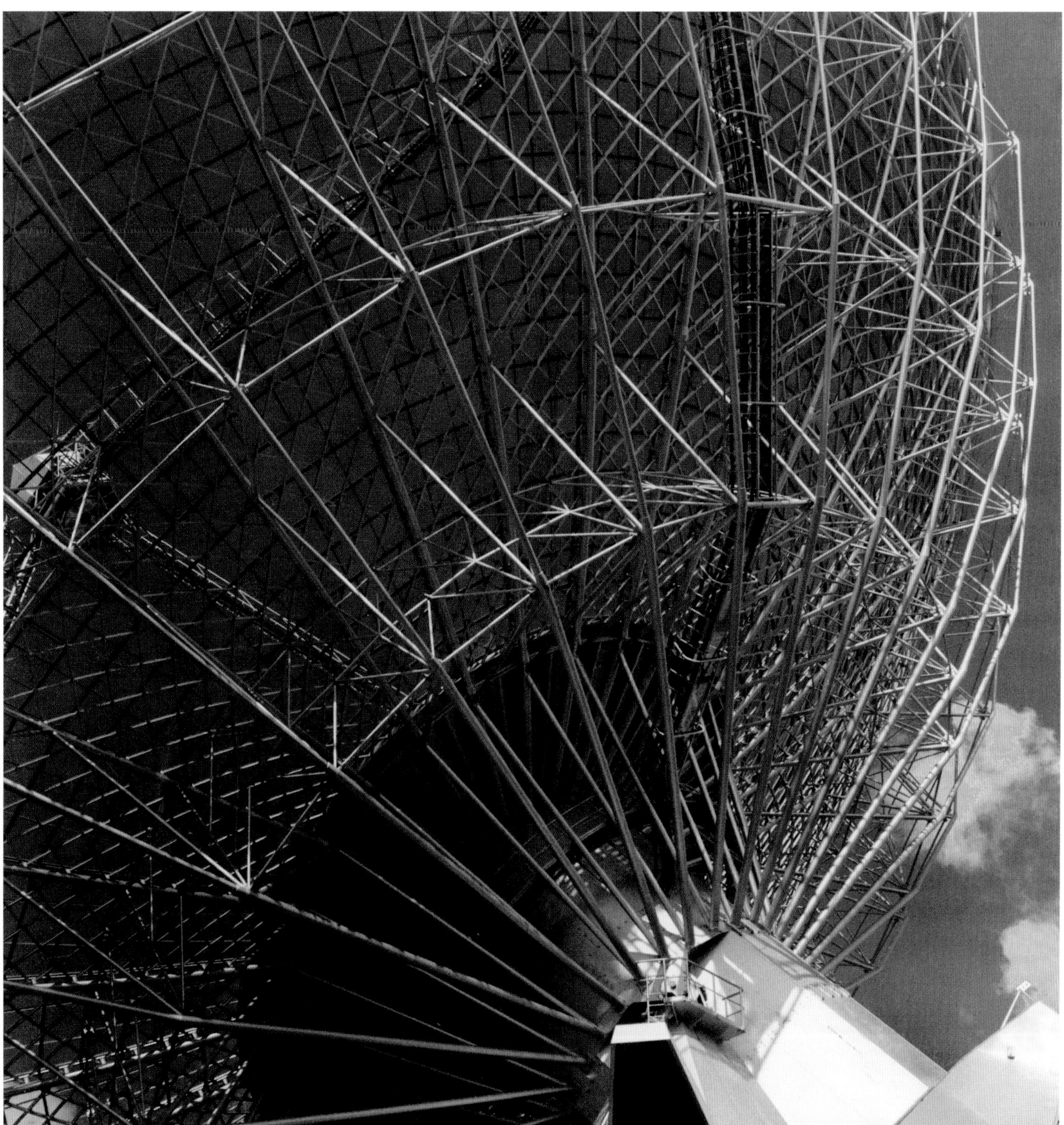

Radio telescope 1963

When I saw the radio telescope at Parkes, in New South Wales, I was excited by its perfect parabolic symmetry. I took several photographs of it from different angles, some with dramatic clouds. This picture was my final selection because I felt that the light glinting on a few parts of its intricate structure emphasised a feeling of delicacy and strength. I think the mathematics of this telescope also appealed to me, imagining all the parallel radio beams from infinity bouncing off the sides of the parabola to meet at its focus where I assumed that the receptive instruments were placed. (I was teaching mathematics at Cowra High School at this time!)

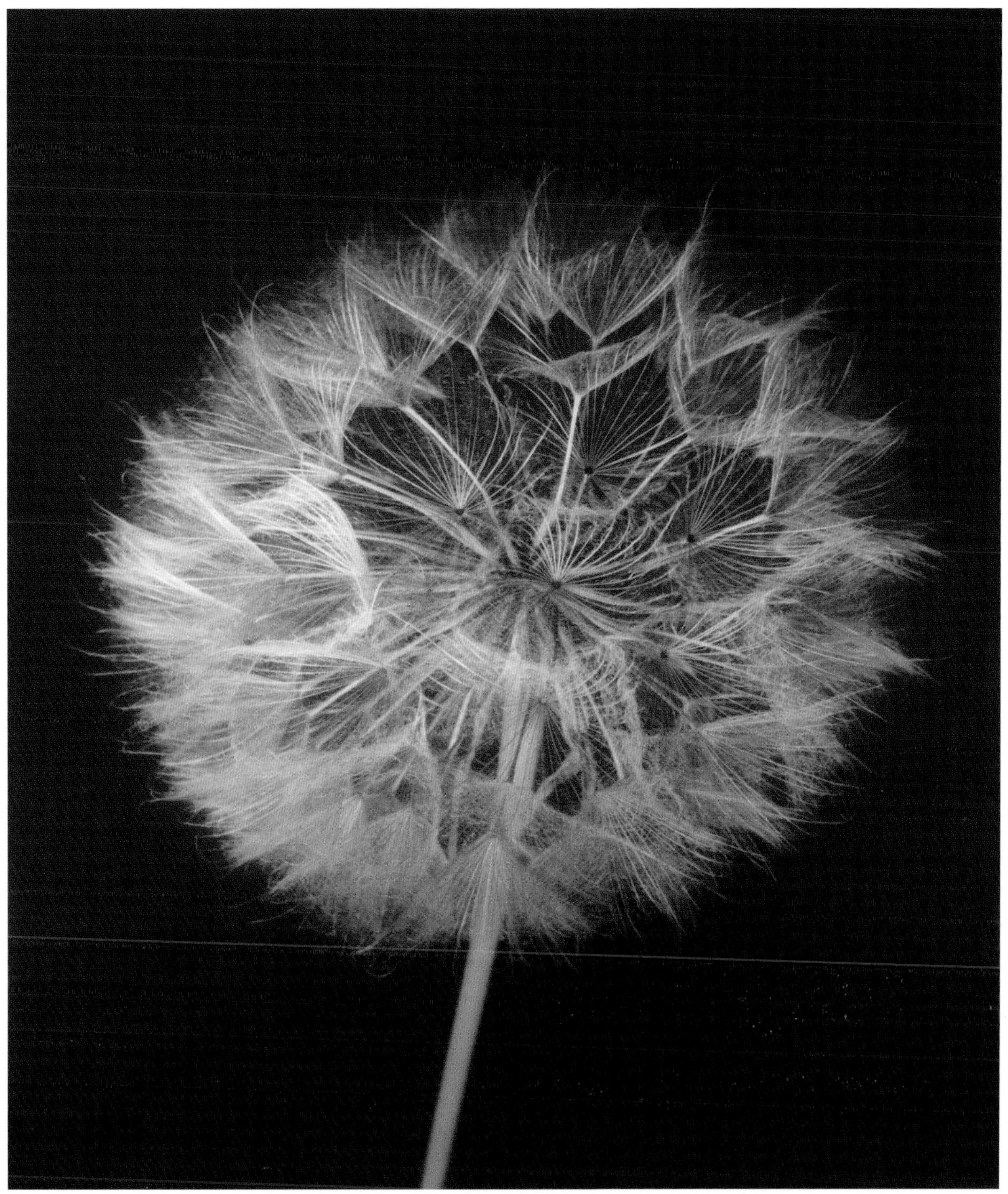

Seed head 1990

Ross brought home a seed head like this one to show me, but it was slightly damaged and hence not a good subject for a photograph. However, he planted the seeds, and then we forgot about them. Two years later when weeding the garden, I found this wonderful seed head. It was nine centimetres in diameter and its beautiful, delicate and intricate symmetry, composed of myriad parts, was breathtaking. I picked it with the greatest care, set it up before a black background and used a small low floodlight to show all its perfect detail. Although we planted its seeds, not one ever produced another plant.

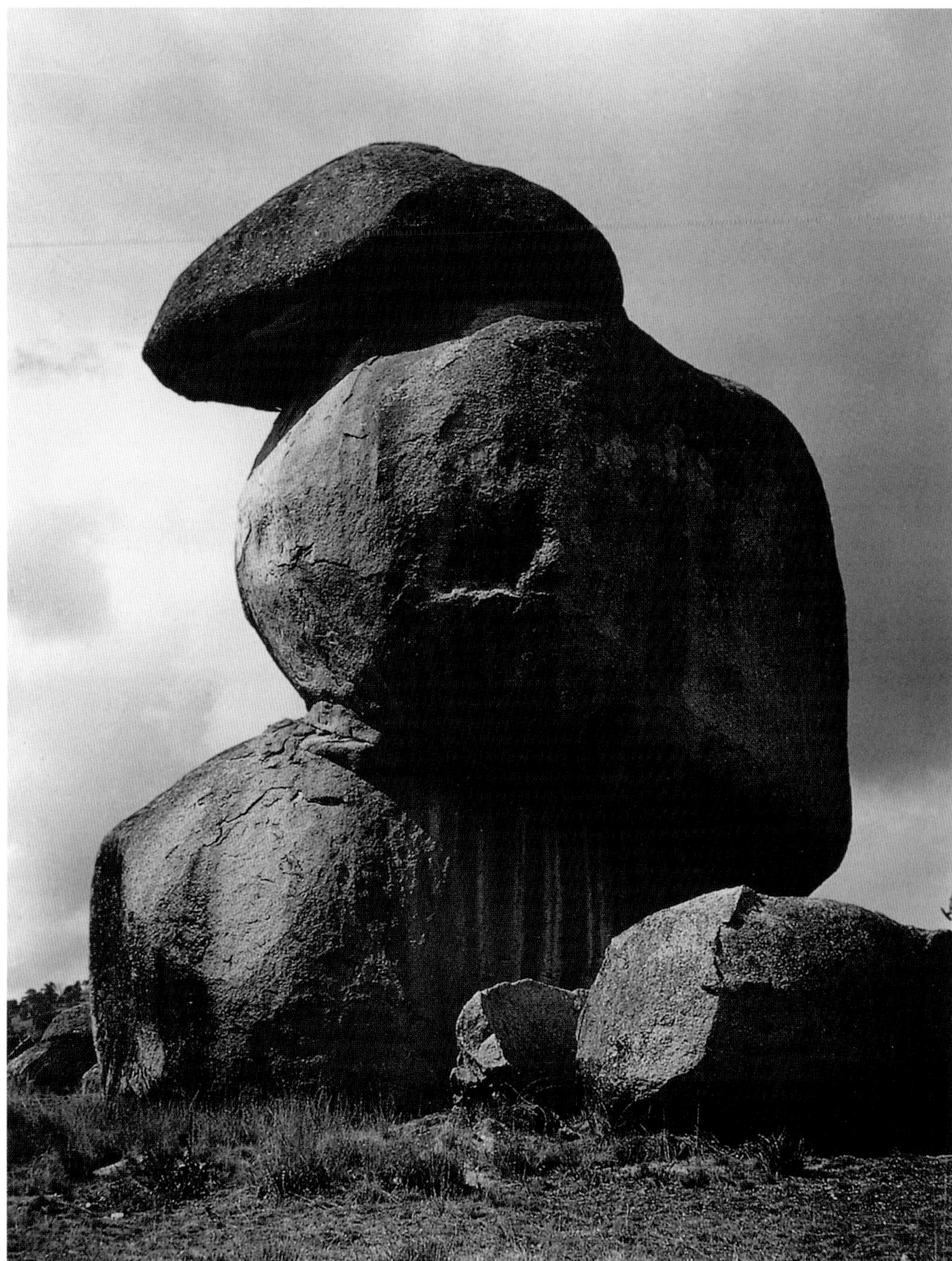

Granite tor 1937

This magnificent tor, which seemed to possess a calm, brooding quality, proved irresistible to my geologist father as well as to me. We climbed through a wire fence, trespassing on private property, to get a closer view. He carried his geological hammer (to get a small specimen from one of the low rocks nearby) and I walked round the tor with my camera to choose the best viewpoint.

My final selection included the small figure of my father, with the hammer raised in his hand, but when I made a print of it the figure seemed to diminish the atmosphere of brooding solitude, so I made another print of the tor alone, and the difference in feeling was surprising. I did leave in the hammer's edge at the right-hand side of the print—for sentiment's sake.

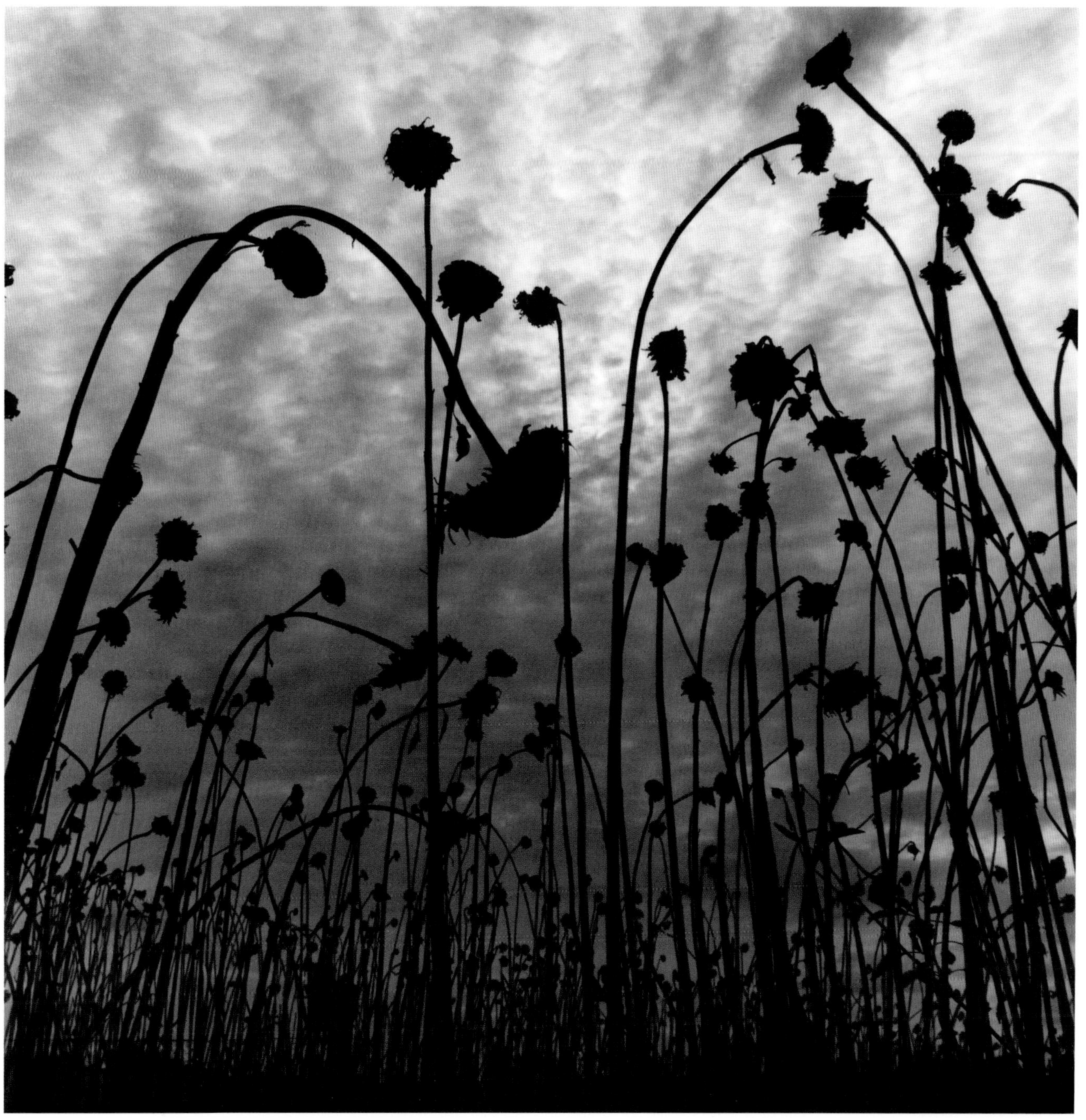

Dead sunflowers 1984

[National Gallery of Australia]

Ross had planted a few rows of giant sunflowers at the edge of our garden, and after the flowers died the seed heads had been left to ripen and were much sought after by birds. When eventually he was ready to cut them down, I, who for some days had been considering their photographic possibilities, asked him to leave them until an interesting sky might provide a suitable background. Finally the hoped-for sky developed and I spent a long time moving amongst the tall dry stalks to select a viewpoint. From about ten different proofs I chose this one, taken with my camera almost at ground level. I'm glad we waited for the right sky.

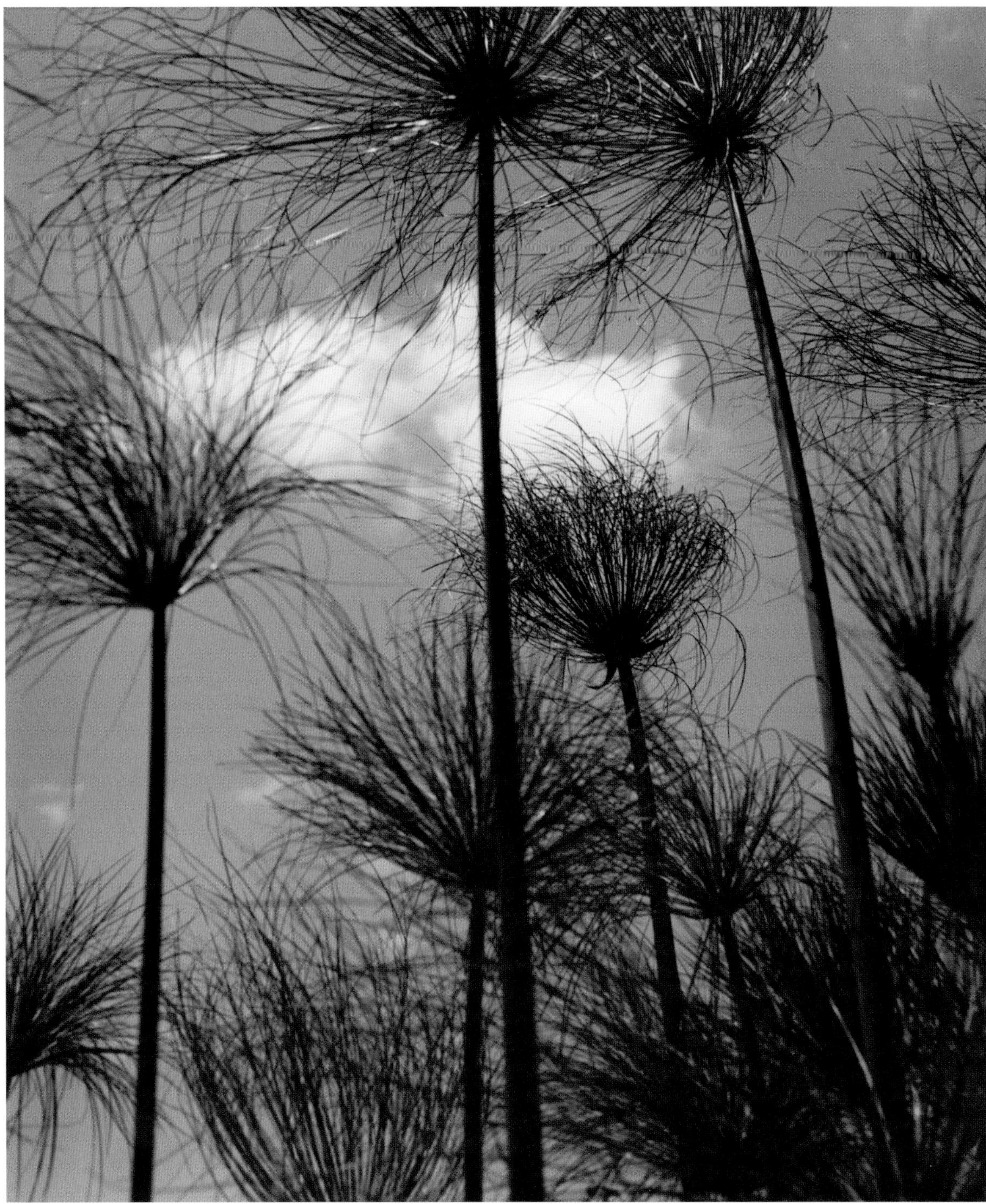

Papyrus 1938
In the Sydney Botanic Gardens I came across a clump of papyrus by a pool. It was a breezy summer afternoon with white clouds drifting by and sunlight glinting on the waving fronds of the plants. I selected a low viewpoint for my chosen group of stalks, and waited patiently until the wind blew a white cloud into place behind them.

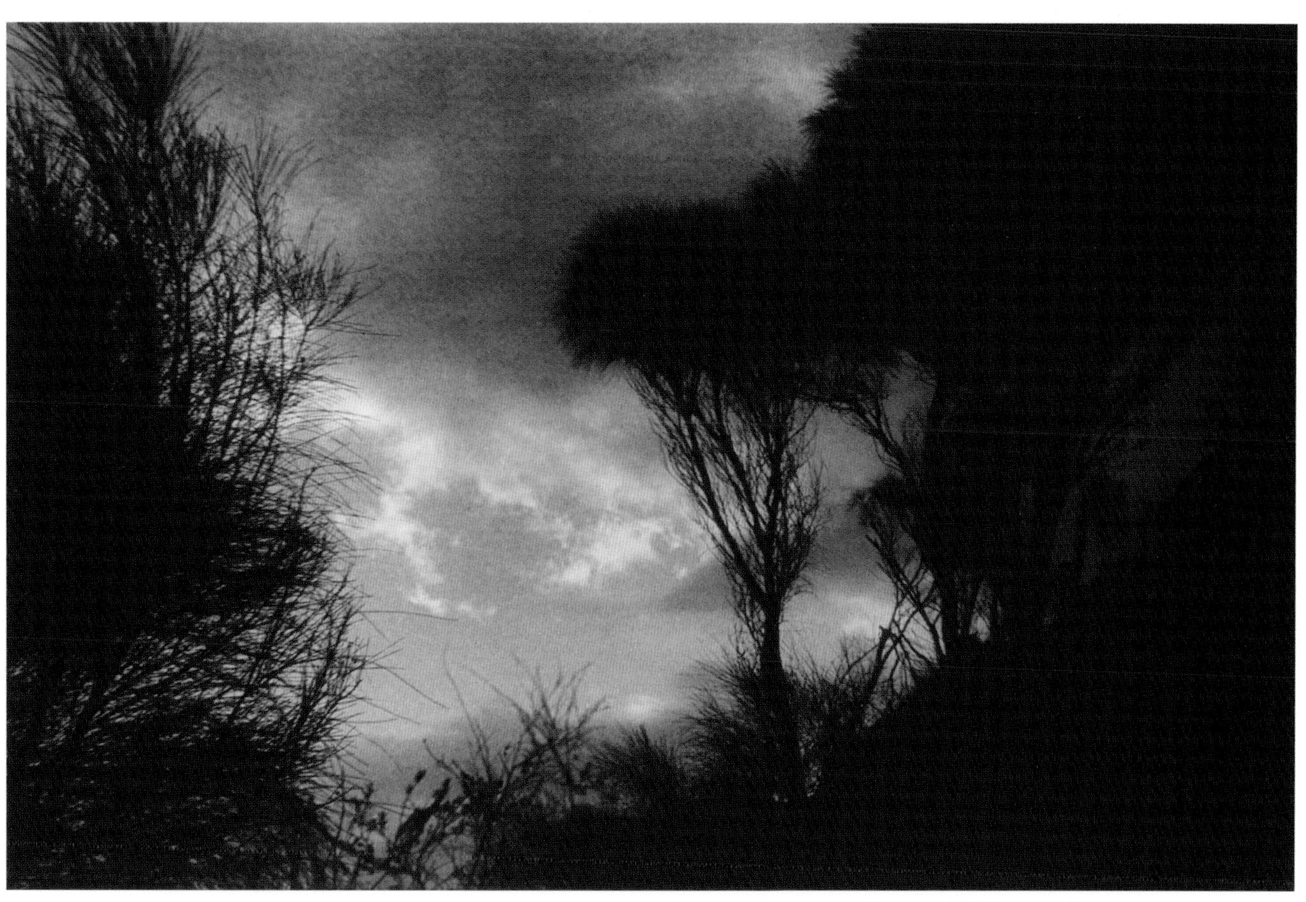

She-oaks 1928

One of my father's brothers, Max, coached medical students in a city building where rooms were also rented by George Dupain, who was an expert on nutrition and physical education. George and my uncle Max became good friends and our families took their annual Christmas holidays at Newport Beach for many years. During Christmas 1924 I first met Max Dupain. We were both interested in photography (though he had a more sophisticated camera, with a bellows) and we could roam all around Newport together taking pictures. These she-oaks were growing, with many others, on Bungan Head at the south end of Newport Beach. I had often walked amongst them with my camera, and chose to photograph this uncomplicated group framing the open sky. I still hear the gentle soughing of the wind through their branches. When I went to live in the country years later I was delighted to find wild she-oaks growing there.

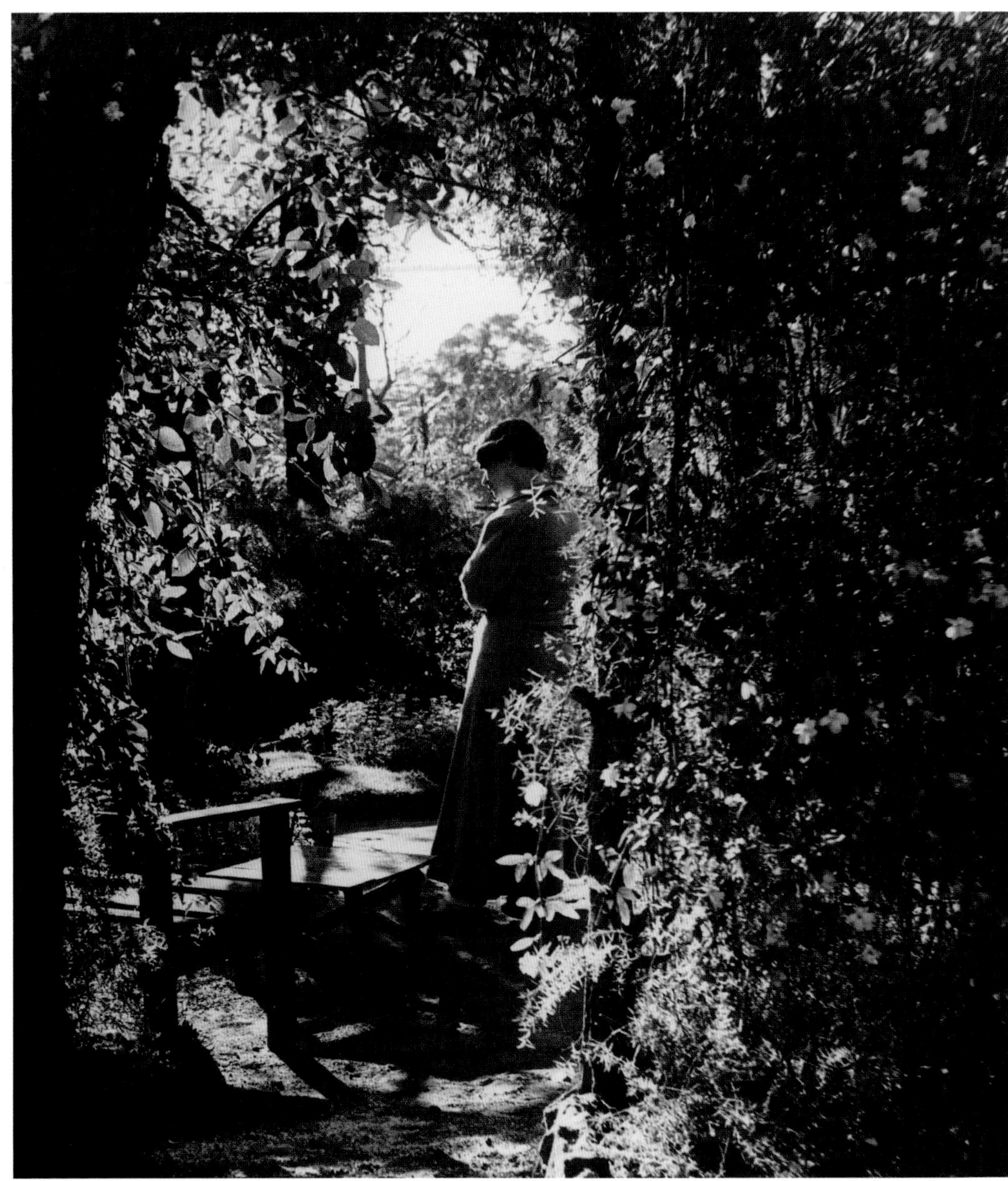

Morning 1946
[National Gallery of Australia]

Ross McInerney and I married late in 1944, just before he was sent overseas with the AIF. When the war ended Ross assumed that he would leave the country and come to the city so I could continue my career, but I took it for granted that I would go with him to live in the country. Max, meanwhile, had returned from the war to take over the running of the studio again, and I was ready for a new life with Ross.

Our first home was a tent in the hills of the Illunie Range south of Cowra, separated from the town by forty-five kilometres of rough dirt roads—not very negotiable in an emergency! I wanted to be near hospital for the birth of my first child, and had been invited down from my country home to stay with my friend Olga Sharp and her kind elderly parents at Wahroonga. (The hospital was a large converted house at Hornsby, which had once been the home of my maternal grandparents. Now a shopping mall stands upon its site.)

I took this photograph of Olga in her garden during my 'waiting' days. The morning light was beautiful.

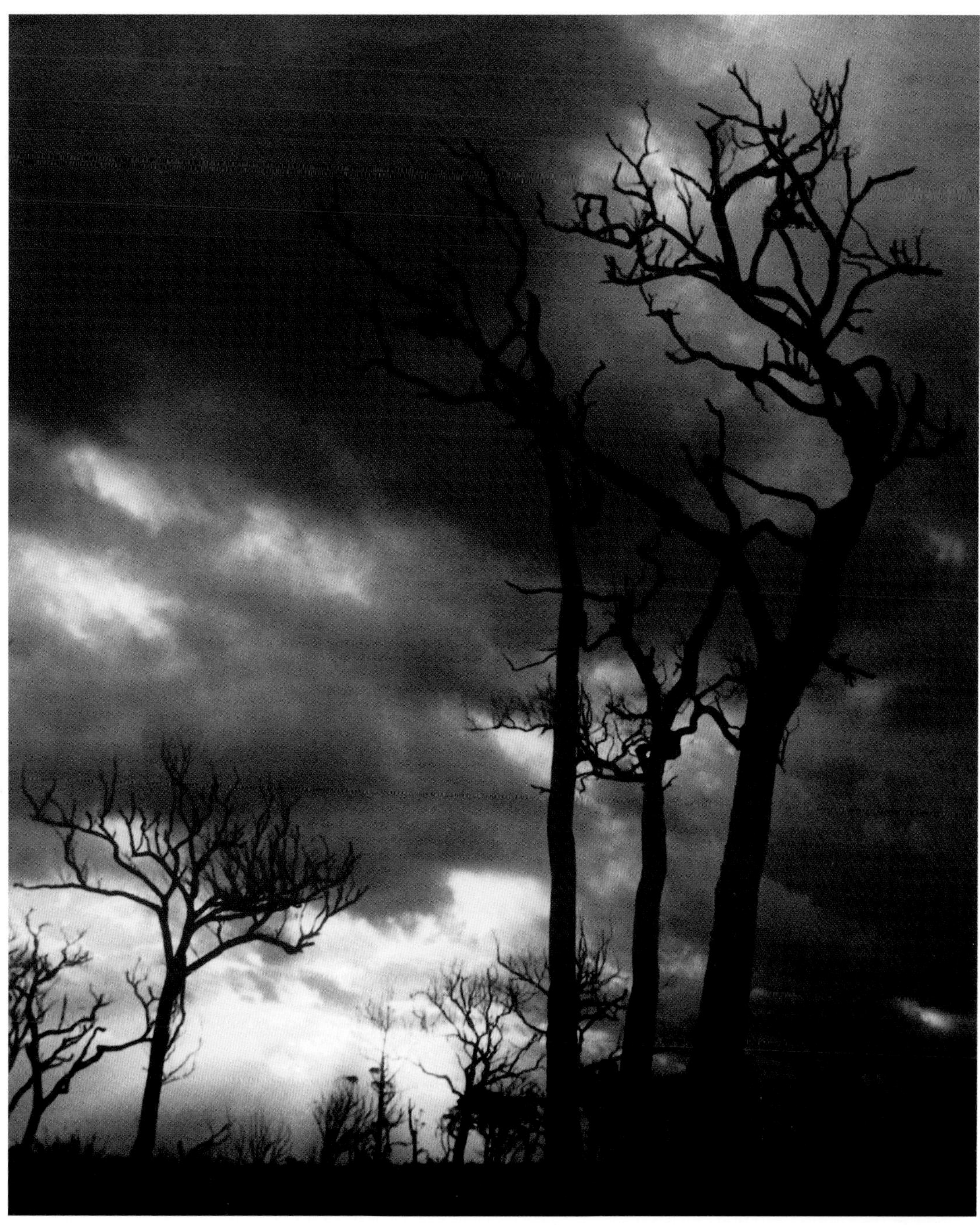

Storm c.1935
These stark, dead trees seem to be leaning against the approaching storm and add to the threatening atmosphere.

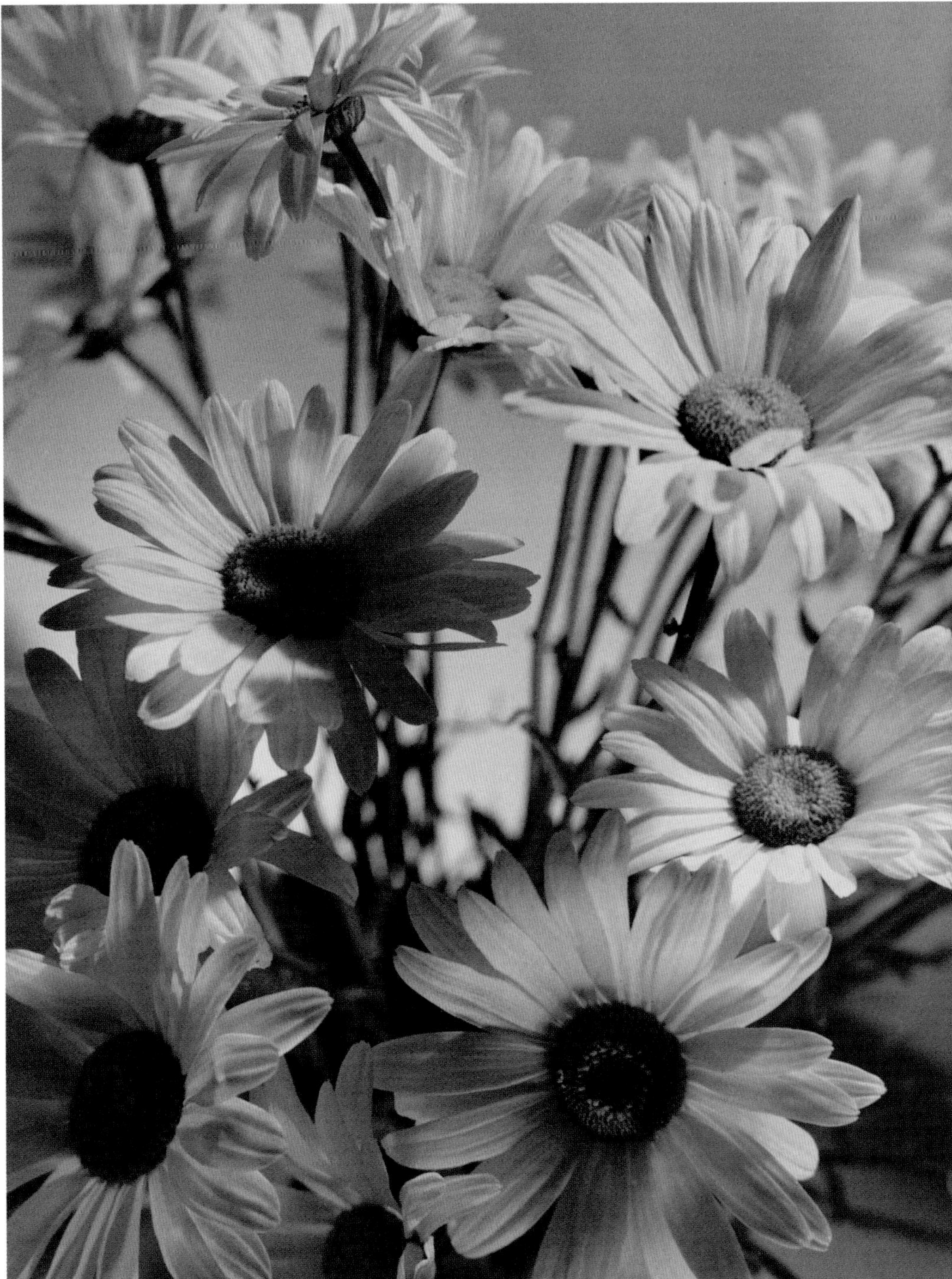

Shasta daisies 1937

[National Gallery of Australia]

I have always been fond of flowers with the simple daisy form, and I chose to photograph these in the studio because out-of-doors I would have had less control of the lighting and background. I examined the composition very carefully through the studio camera's large ground glass focussing screen and—the view from the camera's position being slightly different to my own—made as many rearrangements to the flowers as seemed necessary. I then used (apart from a background light) one source of light to try and convey a feeling of out of doors.

This photograph, with *Winter willows*, was exhibited in the London Salon of Photography in 1937.

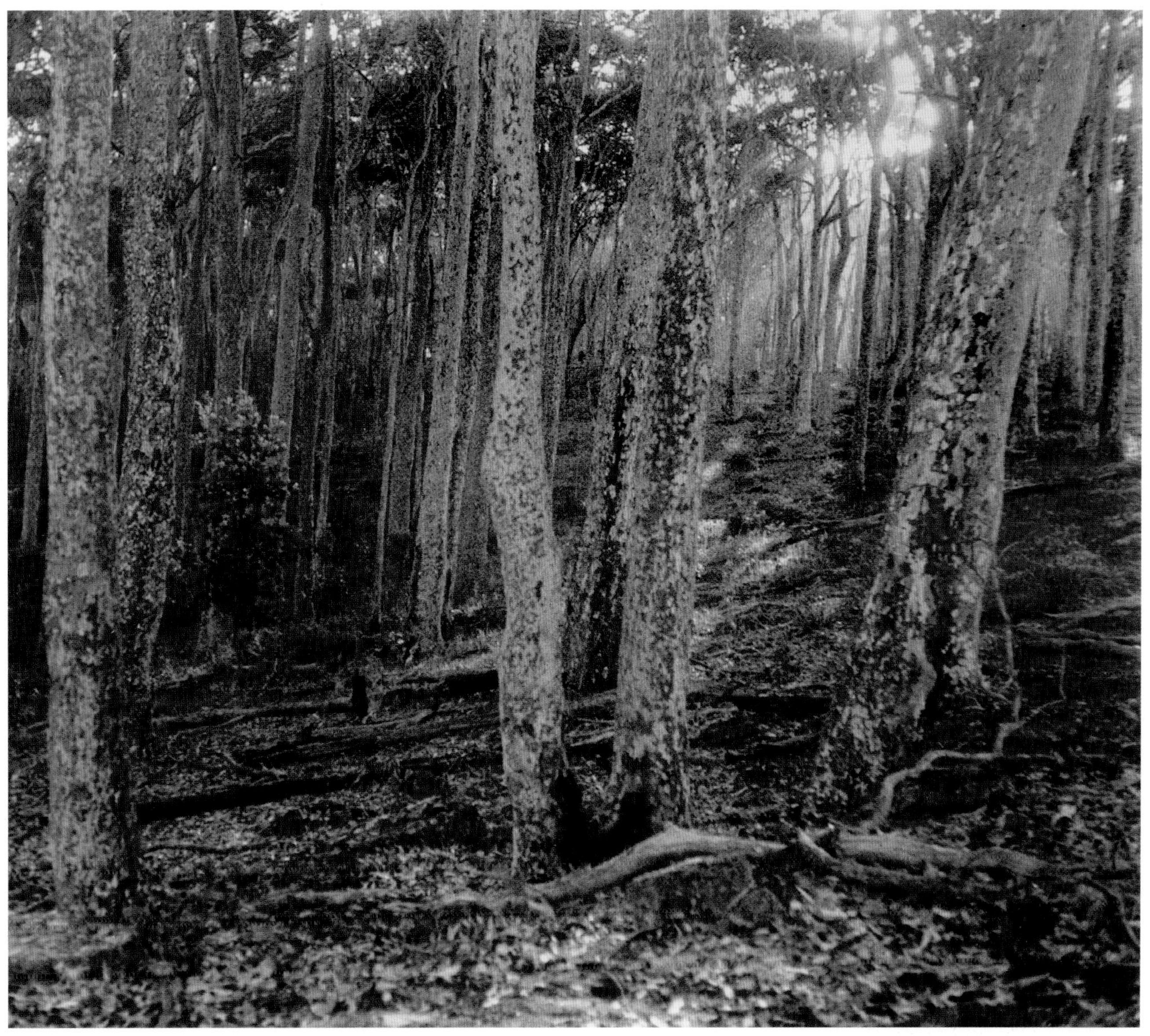

The way through the trees 1938
These beautiful spotted gums (*Eucalyptus maculata*) were at Ulladulla on the south coast of New South Wales. With the shaft of light penetrating their shadowy fastness, they were irresistible.

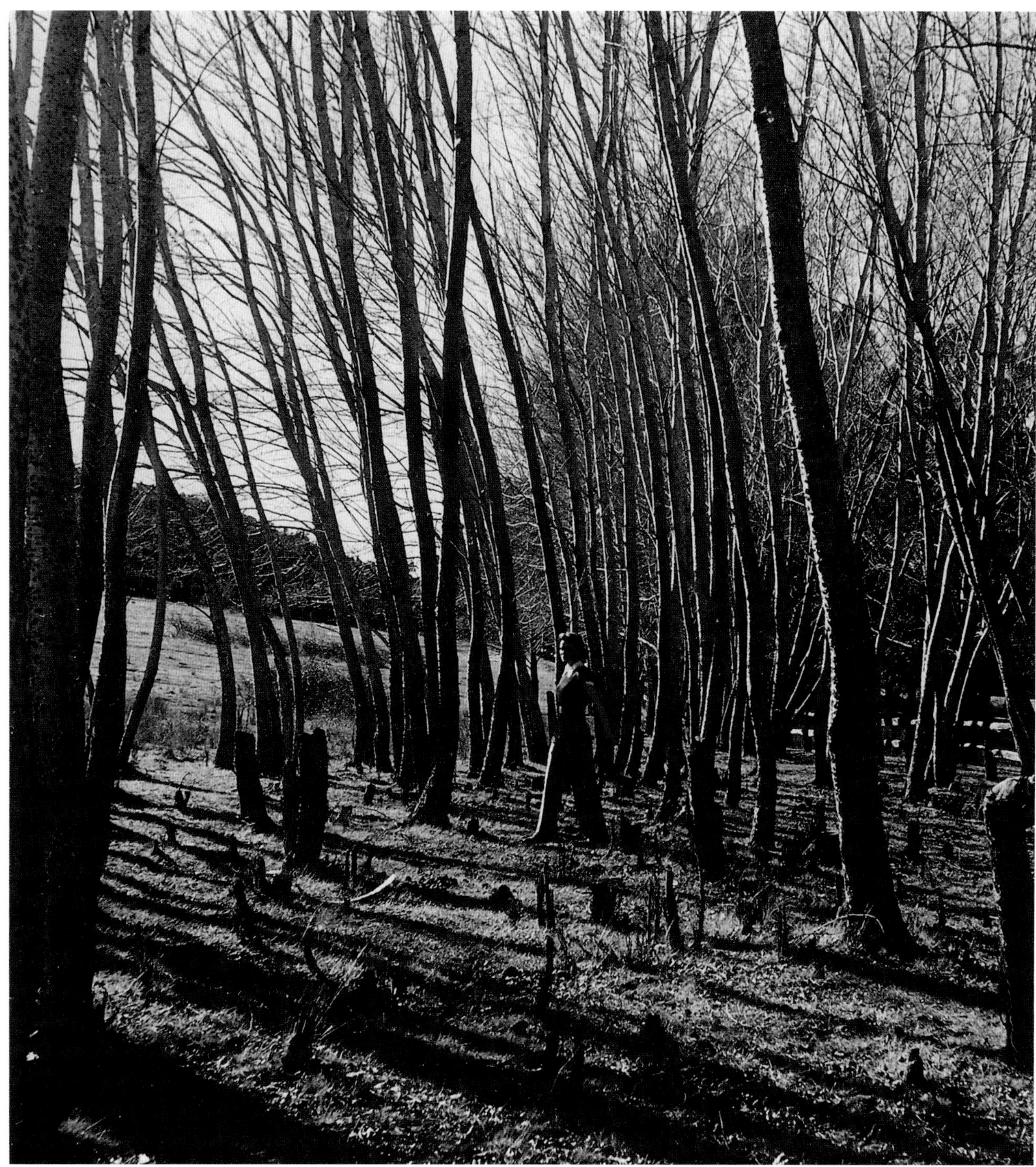

Among the beeches c.1939

The young woman in this photograph is Jean Lorraine. I had seen a photograph of her in the *Women's Weekly* and had suggested to Max Dupain that she might like to do some modelling work for us. She came to the studio and became a very good friend of both Max and myself. If you look closely at the right-hand side of this picture, you will see the crouching figure of Max taking a photograph among these beeches too.

It was the profusion of tree trunks all leaning in the same direction and casting their parallel shadows that appealed to me.

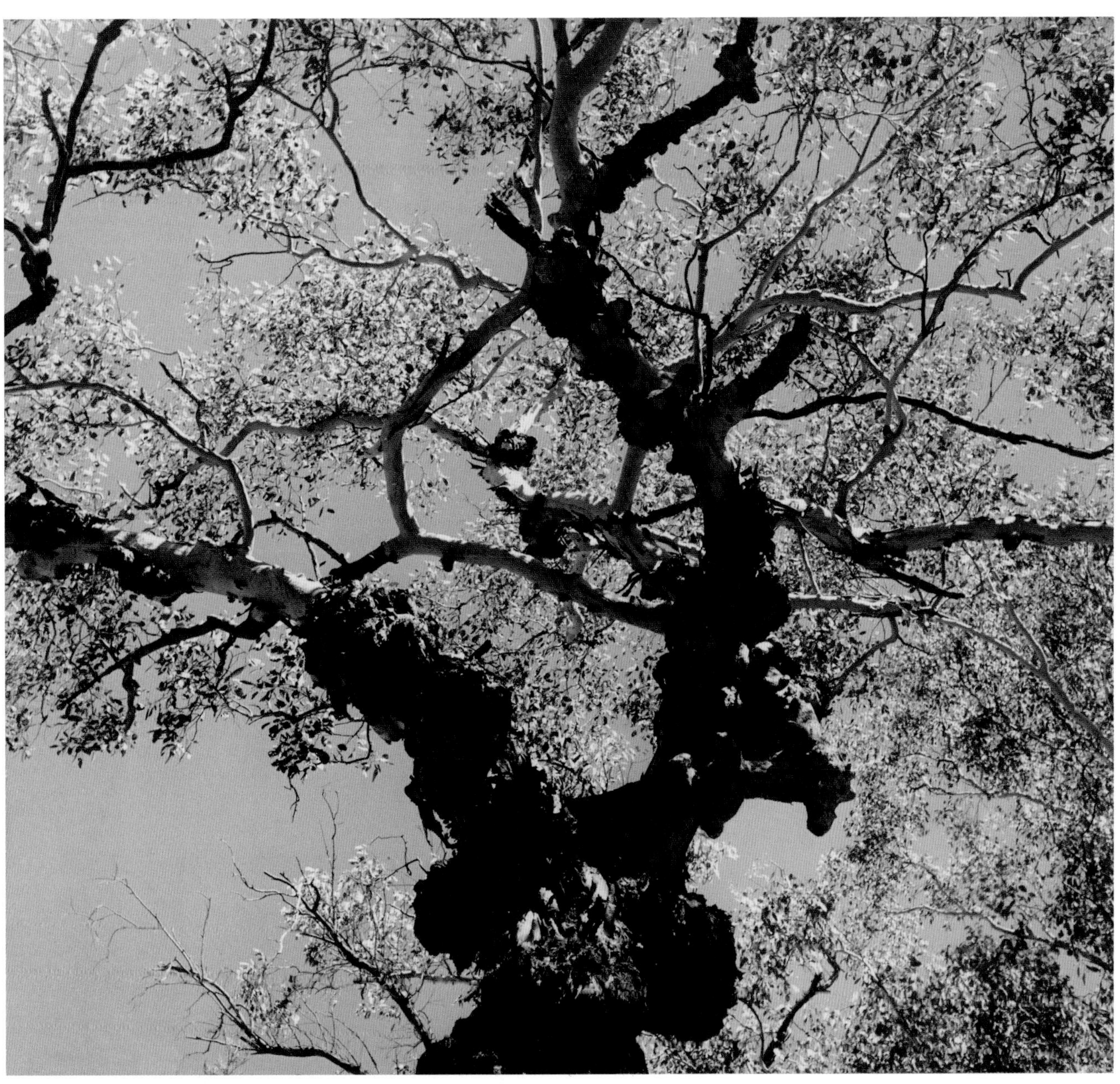

The sunlit tree 1946
This old tree bore a profusion of fresh young leaves backlit by the low sun, as if rejuvenated by the light.

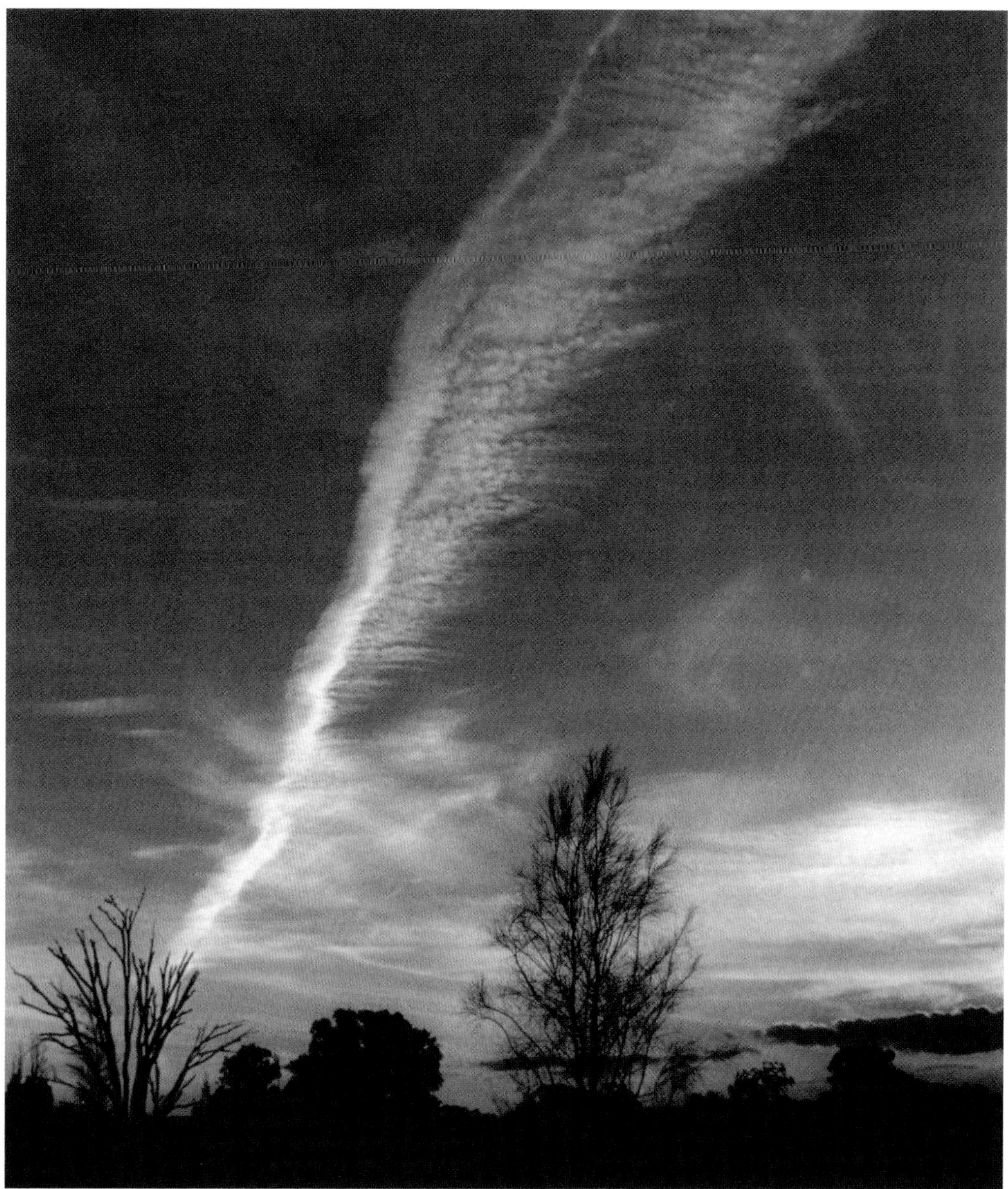

Vapour trail 1991

I had often watched vapour trails criss-crossing overhead, as several air routes pass high over Spring Forest, but it was hard to compose a satisfactory picture of them in just an airy, empty sky. On this occasion a jet had headed over to disappear behind a hill, and by the time I got my camera ready the oldest part of its trail, blown by the wind, had feathered out—and this, together with a narrow foreground of trees, gave stability to the composition.

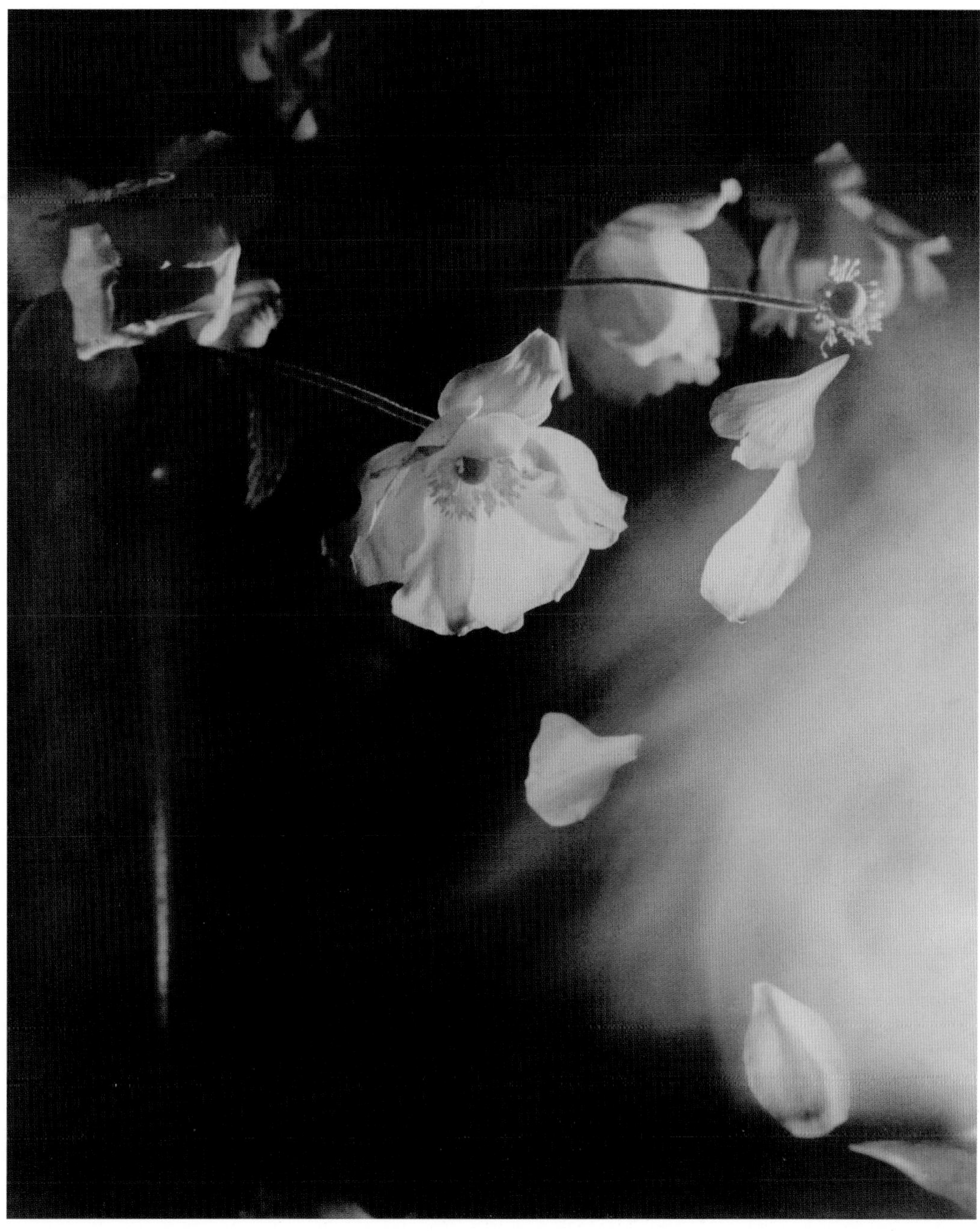

Windflowers 1939

[National Gallery of Australia]

I have always been fond of these single white flowers with their beautiful stamens and their poetic common name. I wanted to suggest a sense of wind movement, and photographed the flowers with the studio camera using two 6½ × 4½ inch cut films. First I photographed them in a supporting vase and against a black background, which meant that a part of the negative was clear film. Then I placed this negative in reverse in the camera's viewfinder, so that I could see where to place the 'falling' petals (arranged on another black background) and the puff of cigarette smoke (which I blew towards the petals at the moment of exposure), all to be recorded on the second film. I then combined both negatives with their sensitive surfaces face-to-face for maximum sharpness, and had a composite negative ready for printing.

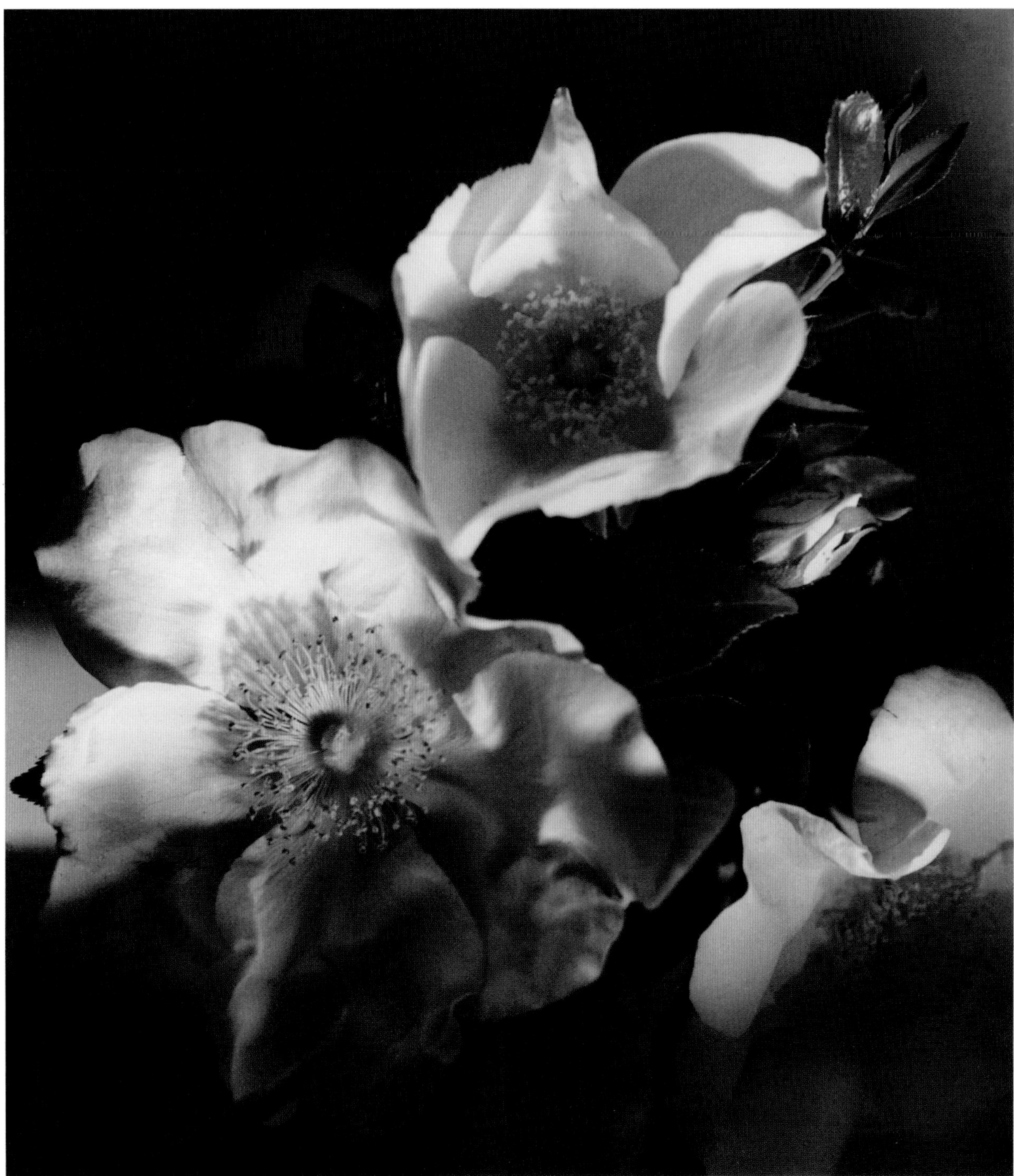

Cherokee rose c.1962

I prefer to photograph simple flowers because their form is more clearly defined, and the Cherokee rose is one of my favourites. This is a five-petalled rose with a central mass of decorative stamens. I made this photograph in my Cowra studio, using a floodlight to control the placing of the light and emphasise the gentle convolution of the petals and their subtle gradations of tone.

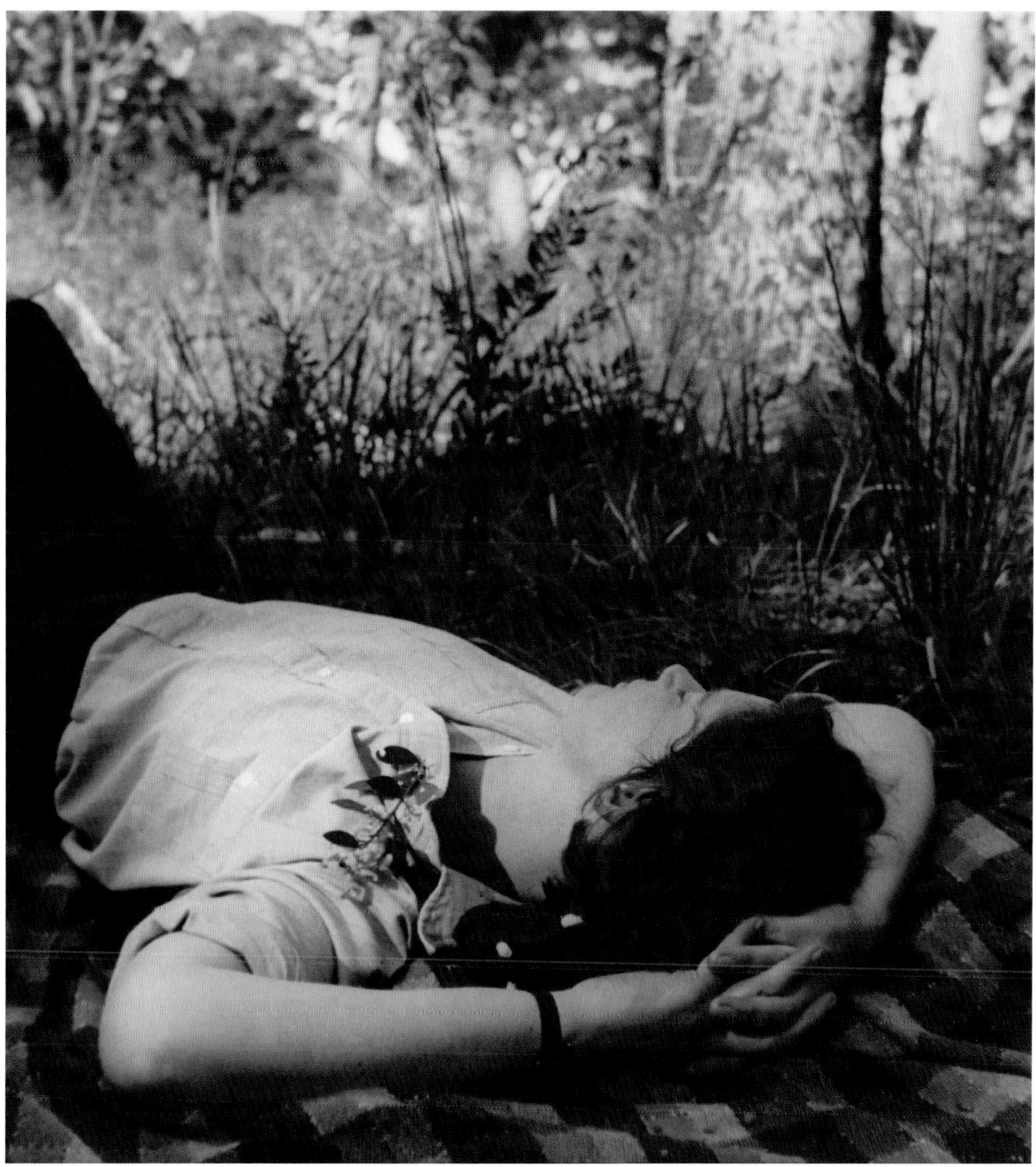

The sleeper 1939

The sleeper was Olga Sharp, a great friend of Max's and mine. We came to know her when she worked in the advertising department of Amalgamated Wireless, and came to the studio when AWA radio sets were sent to us to be photographed for some advertisements. She was interested in all forms of art, especially photography and sculpture, which she studied at Sydney Technical College under Rayner Hoff.

I took this photograph on a bush picnic; Olga stayed behind to rest while I went with the others for a walk. When we came back, there she was, sound asleep on a rug with a wildflower pinned to her blouse, her arms behind her head; and although she was in the shade, the tall grass behind her was brilliant with sunshine. She was a picture of complete relaxation and content in the bush setting which she loved.

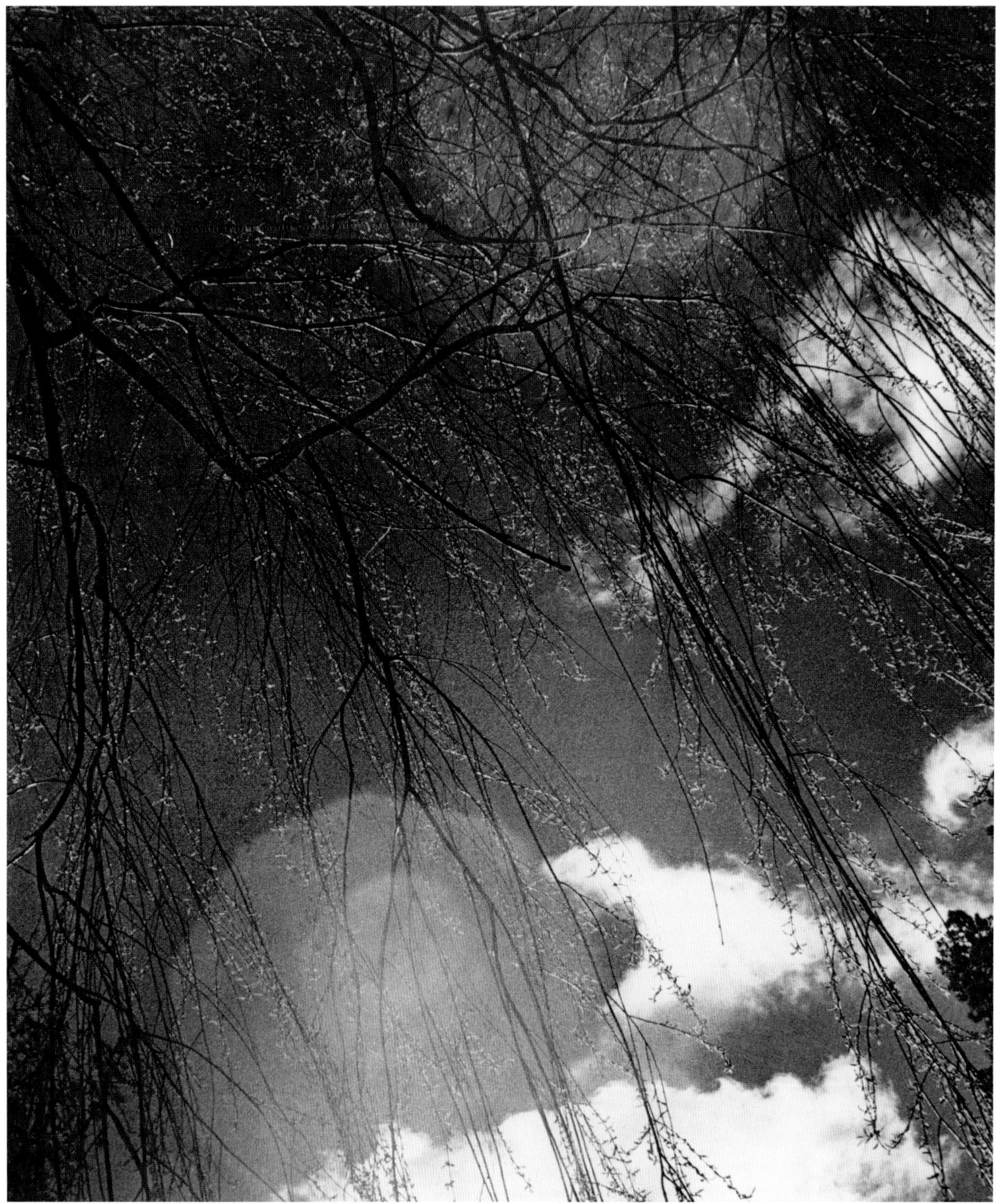

Willow rain 1940
The precise, almost parallel lines of these delicate willow branchlets reminded me of rain falling in a light breeze.

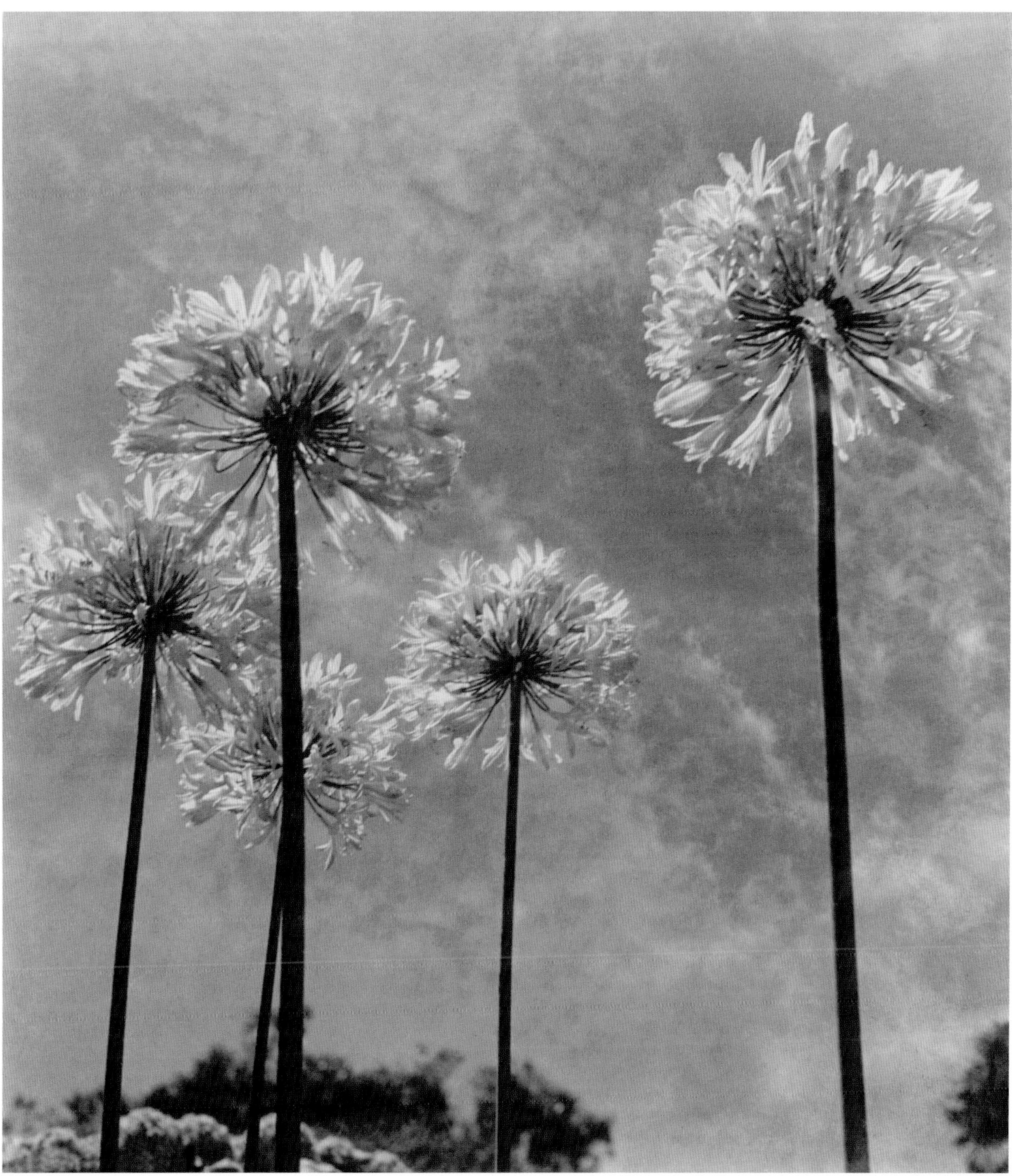

Agapanthus c.1955
For some days I had been watching these large flower heads to see how they looked in different angles of sunlight. I chose to photograph them when the light was catching the tips of all their petals and the low viewpoint showed the dark radiating flower stalks in contrast as well as adding to their stateliness. The sky was cloudless at the time, so for my final print I combined this negative with one of subtle cloud formations.

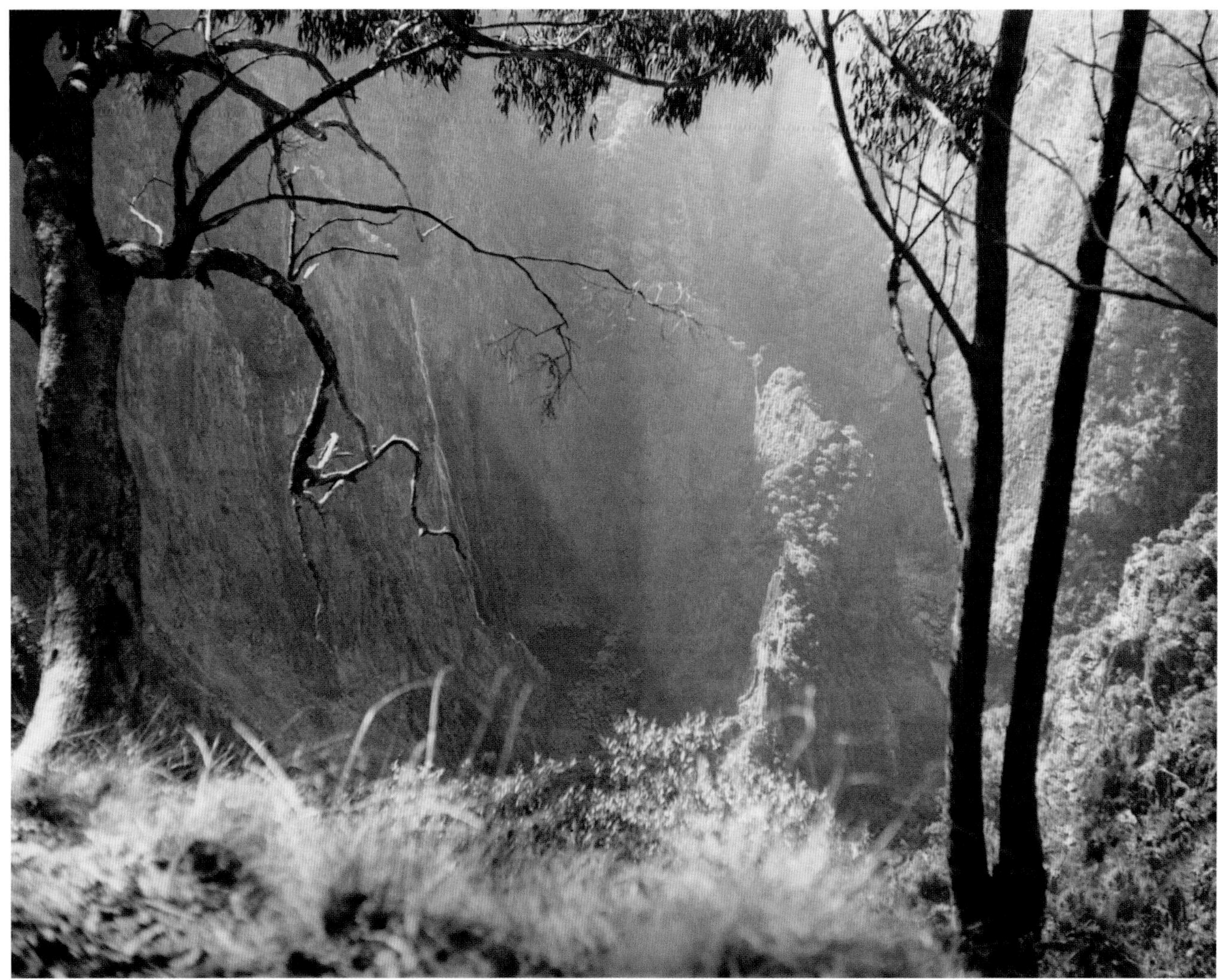

Orchestration in light 1937

On our 1937 overland trip we camped for a night close to the edge of Wollomombi Gorge in the New England tableland. We could hear dingoes calling in the distance all night. I awoke to this wonderful pale early morning sunlight gently touching the protruding rocks and higher levels of the gorge, and I could see the thin stream of a waterfall flowing down to be lost in dark pools in its far depths. There was such a great range of tones, from light through to darkness, that my mind translated it into orchestral sounds, from the high treble of piccolos to the deep sonorous notes of double bass instruments.

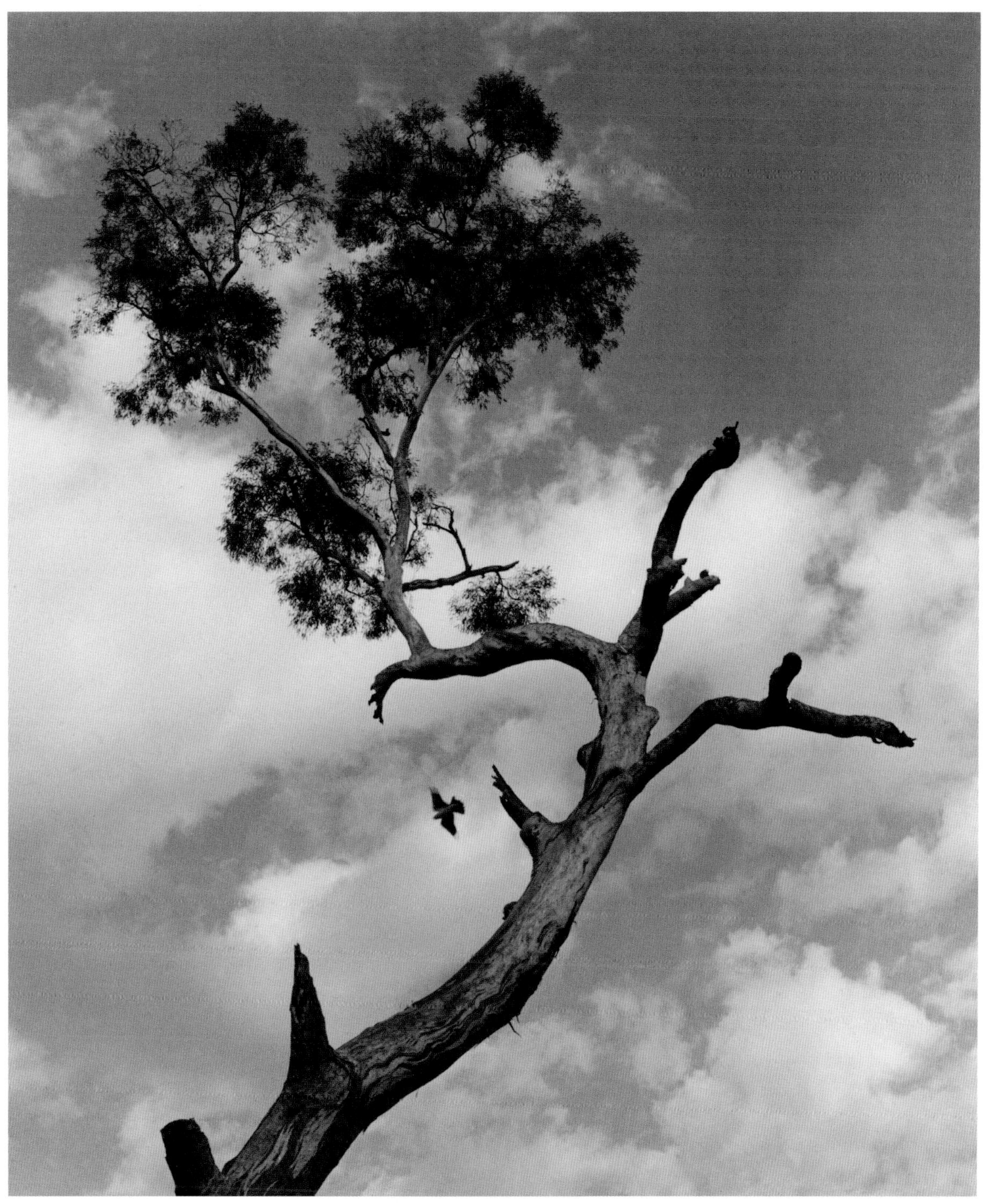

The soaring bird 1993
Over the years, Ross had been observing this tree's struggle to survive, and he eventually took me to see it. The tree had only a cluster of leaves left on its one remaining live branch, and here and there were the hollow remains of former branches, dead and broken. These hollows, however, were nesting places for birds, one of which flew out and went soaring amongst the clouds.

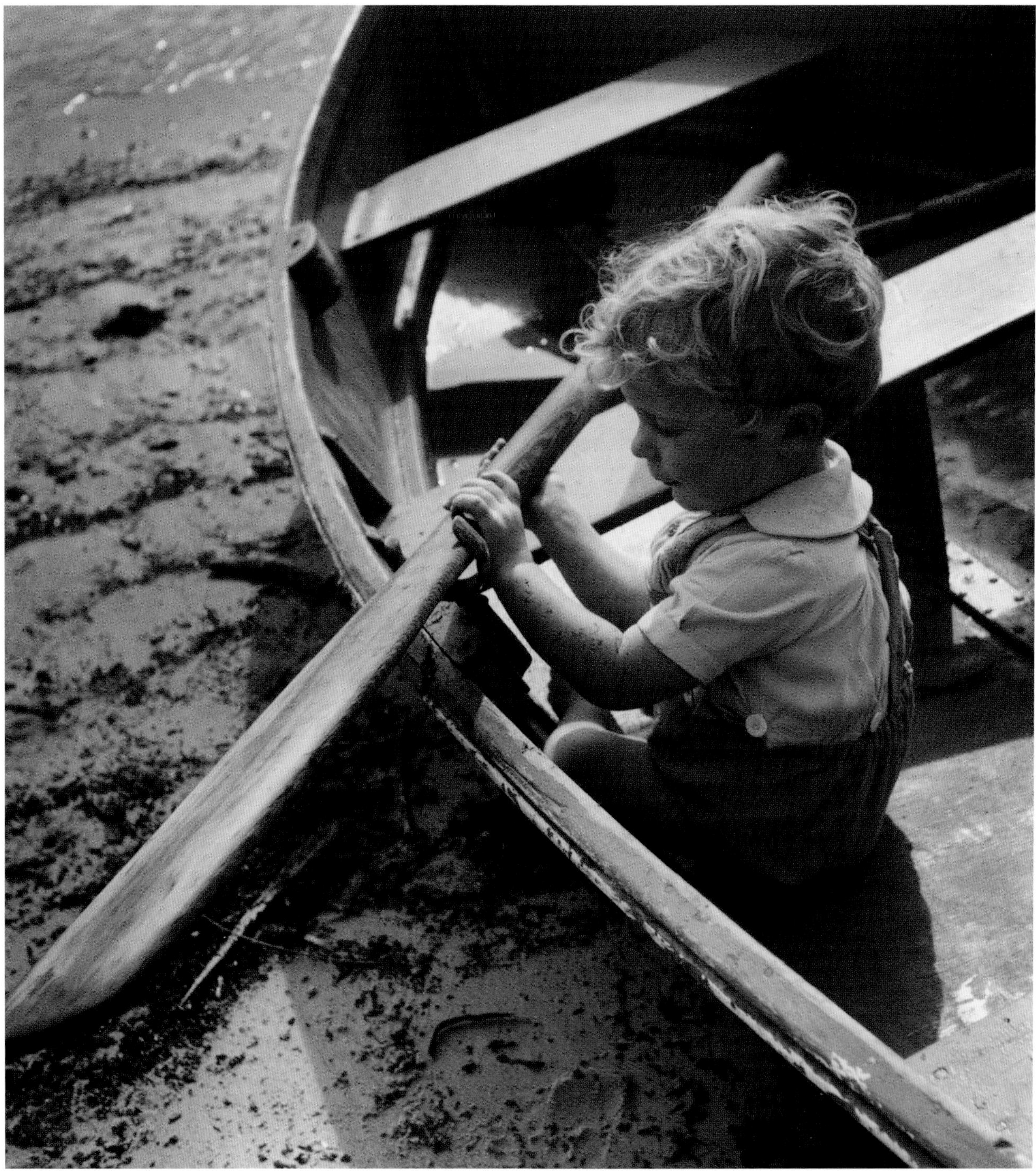

The young oarsman 1949
During the Christmas holidays one year we visited friends at Clareville, on Pittwater, where a rowing boat was beached on the sand. Peter climbed into this boat and was evidently wondering what the oars were for and marvelling at the great expanse of water all around. The only mass of water he had ever seen before was in our country creek.